HOTEL SALES AND REVENUE MANAGEMENT BOOK 2.0

JANUARY 2009

CANADA

HOTEL SALES AND REVENUE MANAGEMENT BOOK 2.0

Carol Verret

iUniverse, Inc.
New York   Bloomington

HOTEL SALES AND REVENUE MANAGEMENT BOOK 2.0

iUniverse books may be ordered through booksellers or by contacting:

iUniverse
1663 Liberty Drive
Bloomington, IN 47403
www.iuniverse.com
1-800-Authors (1-800-288-4677)

ISBN: 978-0-595-51256-0 (pbk)
ISBN: 978-0-595-61825-5 (ebk)

Printed in the United States of America

Contents

Introduction—A Brief History of Time in The Hotel Industry

So why does the industry need a new hotel sales and revenue management book—because the world of travel and hospitality sales has fundamentally changed.

Once upon a time, salespeople were trained to pick up the phone and dial endless numbers out of endless directories and find the name of the person that was responsible for booking hotel accommodations for that organization. Then they were supposed to pick up the phone again and call that person and say "Hello my name is—with the Wiki hotel" If they were not very good they would then ask "How are you?" It is amazing to me that so few people on the other end of the phone did not reply "Why do you care—you don't know me." Maybe people were nicer then.

After those brutal phone calls, hotel salespeople were asked to go up on the roof of the hotel and look around them (no, I'm not kidding). Every building that they saw from the roof of the hotel was a target for yet another exercise in cold calling—walking up and down the street and into offices asking the same question that they asked on the phone. Now this took a lot more courage than the telephone and the worth of a hotel sales person was sometimes measured in the quality of the buildings they had been kicked out of.

Actually, this was in the world before 9/11 changed everything. Maybe people were not as paranoid and probably not as cranky until the number of hotels and hotel salespeople mushroomed to the point where it was veritable barrage of hotel salespeople cold calling the same person!

Then came the development of the regional and corporate sales offices for hotel companies, management companies and franchise organizations—and all of them had a small army of salespeople! Yes, they were all calling on the same poor travel manager!

Is it any wonder that voice mail became the gold standard! The cold call is pretty much dead now and nobody misses it much—especially the person that was cold called. At about the same time, the internet gained traction and a new methodology of sales was enabled. It was no longer necessary to walk the streets to find out who was in the buildings close by—it was all on the internet via a Google search.

Want to find out who the key contacts are and what the company or organization is about—you guessed it, it's all on the internet because at about the same time it became imperative for every company and organization to have their own web site. Just in case the company in question might have been prone to exaggerating their success a little bit on their web site, platforms like Hoovers came along to keep them honest. A sales person could log onto Hoovers or similar platforms and find out their gross sales year over year, the latest press releases about them and just about the kind of underwear the CEO preferred.

At about the same time, since all of the hotel clients were getting web sites, every hotel decided it had to have a web site—some were better than others. Some were built by the 12 year old child of the GM who was the only one who had a clue how to do it. Others were sleeker, had better photography and had a professional build meta tags so that it could be found on the internet.

However, two little web sites began to get a lot of attention—Travelocity and Expedia. The hotel community hated them but the consumer loved them! There on one page (there weren't that many pages at first and the battle for position had barely begun) were all the hotels in the area that they were travelling to with all of the rates! How cool was that! No calling the travel agent (that's another story), no calling AAA—just click and book.

The hotels were caught by surprise as the travel platforms or what we now refer to as OTAs pulled their inventory and information for the hotels off of the GDS system. The GMs felt that they had lost control over their inventory; the rates they could sell when and the moaning went on and on! However, the OTAs are here to stay, have multiplied and now come in many flavors—want to customize your trip, no problem!

The OTAs became very powerful because as the consumer loved them and as they generated more and more volume for the hotels, the OTAs began raising their commission rates. The pages on the sites multiplied to the point that the OTAs said to the hotel community that if they wanted to be on the first several pages instead of the twentieth, it would cost them more in commission and would require a Merchant Agreement.

Many hotel companies refused and the trend to booking online at the franchise web site was born so that the EVIL OTAs didn't get all the commission, the franchises did! All hotels began to build their own web sites with the capability of taking reservations until their franchises forbade it. Then it became important that the independent hotels have the same functionality on their web sites so that the consumer could book on the site and thereby level the playing field between the franchises and the independents.

Between the search thing and the functionality of booking rooms on the hotel web site, a whole new industry was born called Search Engine Optimization. I digress—back to the point and there is one for hotel sales.

Unfortunately all through this period the prevailing opinion was that the hotel sales person had to make X number of cold calls, etc., etc,. Unfortunately, there are still managers that still believe this. The hotel sales process and the people who evaluate it have been slow to change.

With the shift in internet usage resulting in Web 2.0, hotel review sites have emerged as the heavy hitters in the decision making processes of both consumers and meeting planners. The OTAs always had reviews on their respective sites but it wasn't until Trip Advisor emerged as the premium consumer generated review site that consumer generated reviews began to get traction as a major force in the hotel sales process, both for transient leisure business and for meeting planners.

Revenue management matured as discipline and we began to understand just how much money hotels had been leaving on the table all of these years. Many hoteliers instinctively thought that this was the case but the revenue management models were finally able to demonstrate it. Revenue management rapidly moved from Excel spreadsheets to highly sophisticated programs driven by complex algorithms that allowed hotels to not only manage but predict demand more accurately.

The roles of revenue management and hotel sales are interdependent and complimentary—although at one point there was a great deal of tension between them. The revenue manager is now picking up some functions that were previously associated with sales such as completing the RFPs for the travel agent consortia who continue to be players.

This brings us to the recent past and the present, an exciting time to be in sales and revenue management. I decided to compile this book of many articles that I have written and new chapters that I have added. I have been contributing articles to Hotel Online since Carol Verret Consulting & Training was founded. However, because I am published primarily online there is a large chunk of the industry that hasn't read my stuff with my take on the new paradigm of hotel sales Web 2.0— that's why I decided to publish this book online and in print version.

This is only the beginning of exciting changes for hotels sales. Because of the unique dynamic between the internet and hotel distribution, hotel sales processes have been impacted more profoundly than the sales processes in many other industries. Hold on for the ride—it's going to continue to morph. Have fun!

Hotel Sales

Web 2.0 and the Hotel Sales and Revenue Management Processes

Web 2.0 is a shift in the way we use the internet. It began with Google and search, the rise of Wikipedia and 'wikis' that led to blogs, open source software, etc. The user took control of their internet experience and contributed to the content on the web. This is an oversimplification but the hotel industry in particular and the travel industry in general were in prime position to be heavily impacted by Web 2.0.

The OTAs and Google search had already fundamentally changed the way customers located, qualified and purchased hotel rooms. The advent of Trip Advisor and other review sites put control firmly back in the hands of the customer. They didn't need to believe the copy in hotel marketing brochures they could check out the experiences of others who had stayed there.

As if the written reviews were not enough, it became possible to upload pictures of hotels, many of which contradicted the pictures in those marketing brochures. Is it any wonder that Seth Godin wrote All Marketers are Liars—it reflected the opinion of a consumer that now had control and no longer had to buy into the hype generated by the marketing departments? Suddenly, hotels had to listen and pay attention to the consumer who could make or break a hotel with a review and a few pictures or a video.

Web 2.0 has fundamentally changed the hotel sales and revenue management processes. The hotel sales department is now picking up the consumer later in the process. Professional meeting planners now have access to RFP platforms from which they can draw database of hotels and solicit all of them with one RFP. They then wait for the responses and pick and choose those from which they want to select. Web 2.0 in action!

Very few people now call or email a hotel that they haven't checked out on the internet. They are not using the Yellow Pages!

Revenue managers now have to manage something we call the hotel's internet presence that includes not only those internet pieces designed and placed by the hotel such as the web site, they also have to monitor the reviews sites. If they employee a sophisticated system, they have access to the web presence of their competitors as well.

The article elaborates on the impact that Web 2.0 has had on the hotel sales process.

Web 2.0 and Hotel Sales Strategies for '08—What are Your Clients Saying about You?

So you think your clients aren't out there talking about you? You think that clients and potential clients don't exchange their thoughts about the experiences they have had at your hotel? Think again!

If the term Web 2.0 has you scratching your head, you are not alone. However, it is important that hotel sales departments get up to speed on the concept. Web 2.0 is the trend to User Generated Content, that is, the use of social networking, hotel review sites and blogs dealing with the user experience.

Sales and marketing strategic plans for '08 that ignore this shift in travel marketing do so at their own peril. A PhocusWright study earlier this year that indicated small group travel such as weddings, family reunions, etc. will be dominated by web based sourcing and booking of room blocks. This was just given additional credibility with the launch of Priceline's new group travel functionality.

Travelocity just launched a new review functionality on its site that will allow users to sort through reviews by destination interest and travel preferences so that there is no need to wade through all of the reviews to locate the ones that pertain to a shopper's travel preference. A Yahoo study last week revealed that travel reviews are driving buying decisions more than price.

How do you plug into and take advantage of this seismic shift in the world of hotel sales and develop strategies for success in this arena for 2008?

- **Design a strategy for the hotel's online presence**. As part of the sales and marketing plan for '08, develop a strategy with Action Plans to monitor and influence the online presence of the hotel. Evaluate it through the eyes of a potential travel and meeting planner. There are products out there to assist you such as Chatter Guard that will monitor every new online review and reference to the property. A cheaper alternative is to set Google alerts which are free and will alert you with an email you every time your hotel is mentioned in an online review, blog or other online media.

- **Hotel Web Site and Property Descriptions**. Review the web site with the eyes of the travel planners and meeting planners. Expedia states that for every dollar spent on their site another dollar is spent on the property web site. If you have a franchise site, ensure that you are changing up your property screens to reflect market segment seasonality for transient travelers and good information for meeting planners. Remember, this is often the first contact that the planner has with your hotel.

- **Online RFPs**. If you participate in an online RFP site such as Star Cite among others, review how you are presenting your property on the sites and the way the sales department responds to RFP request. Participate in the small group planning sites such as Travelocity, Groople, Hotels.com, etc. Again, ensure that you have listed the amenities that are important to these small social groups. Check out the sites for the competitions' amenity profiles and rates. Put an online RFP page on your web site. (Stay tuned for another article on this subject).

- **Respond to Online Reviews**. Instead of just groaning about a negative review, evaluate them as to the validity of their issues. If it is an operational deficiency, bring it to the attention of operations so it can be addressed. Respond to the review in a balanced and professional way that indicates you listen to your customers' comments and respond to their concerns. Yes, there are the 'wacko' reviews about stupid stuff beyond your control, but the customers that are checking out the review sites are usually smart enough to factor those out.

- **Participate in the Chatter**. If organizations and associations that you belong to have a blog, monitor them and post comments—positive and constructive comments. Many

4

local business journals now have blogs as does MPI nationally—your local chapter may have one as well. Build a blog where your clients can give you feedback and you can monitor and participate in online conversations with them.

These suggestions are just a few of the ways to plug into Web 2.0 in your sales and marketing strategies for '08. Your clients live online and how you plug into their concerns and decision making processes will dictate the success of a hotel property. Get on the radar screen!

Web 2.0 is not going away—if anything it will become more important in all travel segments. Ignore it at your peril!

The Habits Of Successful Hotel Salespeople Series

Introduction

The Habits Of Successful Hotel Sales series of articles has been updated every year. It will continue as the processes morph and become more refined. Sales habits are like any other habits. We get up in the morning, take a shower, and brush our teeth almost without thinking about it. That's what successful sales habits are all about.

The things we do when we get to the office and the way we do them in sales should become just like those habits. The morning habits mentioned above are done with a sense of urgency dictated by the time in which we have to do them. So should sales habits be done with the same sense of urgency.

Most hotel salespeople are not paid on a commission basis—if you want to see urgency hang out with and model behavior after those people whose living depends on the habits they implement to sell today! Work as though you were leaving on vacation tomorrow!

See in the next few articles how the habits of hotel salespeople have evolved over the course of several years—they build on each other, not replace each other.

Habits of Highly Successful Hotel Salespeople—A Seismic Shift in 2008!

This annual update of successful habits finds that the process of hotel sales (and hotel sales training that goes with it!) has undergone a seismic shift. If anyone doubts this, read the HSMAI report on the recent hotel sales strategy conference where a panel of meeting and event planners tells hotel salespeople that they had 'better get online for RFPs and bookings'. (HSMAI, 9/07)

"It's not big that eat the small, it's the fast that eat the slow"* applies more than ever—if your salespeople are busy making cold calls to directories and Top 100 lists—you are not on board with the impact of the online space in terms of online RFPS, bookings and user generated content sites like blogs and review sites like Trip advisor.

The fast eat the slow by responding to online RFPs in warp speed, responding to negative reviews on online review sites, managing the hotel's online presence to ensure that the information and rates are transparent across all channels and participating in online RFP sites that are appropriate to the hotel's position in the market. Small group booking sites are increasingly important—both those on the franchise site and the OTA sites.

Effective communication is critical—both email and being able to 'sell' over the phone when a planner finally is reached. A planner on the HSMAI panel indicated that hotel salespeople need to be able to sell over the phone once an RFP has been responded to. After three years of taking orders, telephone selling skills are critical—a hotel sales person may only get one shot at letting a planner know why they should choose their hotel over the rest.

Long term relationships are still the 'best' but the planner is under pressure to put every piece of business out to bid in order to demonstrate the effective use of budget. Building relationships often begins at a later stage in the meeting planning process—the planner has already prequalified the hotel online.

How do these developments impact the habits of hotel sales professionals?

- **Brush up on your and telephone sales skills.** While planners are locating hotels online, the fact remains that we still have to skillfully build a relationship and CLOSE them! Get the sales department some training in telephone sales skills so that regardless of who is communicating there is a skill level and polish that is characteristic of the hotel's sales department. Phone skills that are often neglected include building rapport, qualifying, presenting then closing on the contract or next contact point. Remember—you can 'hear' a smile!

- **The art of effective email communication.** Whether it is in response to an inquiry or an email approach, always put yourself in the position of the recipient. If you were to receive your response, what would you be looking for in a return email? Make it a habit to review your emails for tone, grammar and spelling errors that spell check doesn't catch! Always insert your signature line so that the recipient can find the phone number and web site address.

- **Select RFP sites carefully and by market segment specialization.** Many RFP sites specialize in certain types and quality of property—make sure your property is represented on those that target planners interested in your type of hotel. Don't forget government sites if that is one of your target markets. In the same HSMAI panel discussion, a government planner revealed that they will be expected to use an online RFP site in planning meetings.

- **Establish a process to follow up on RFP requests in hours.** This is sometimes difficult if a hotel sales person is out on the road making calls or at a trade function. Have a designated inside person that monitors all RFP requests from all channels and can respond to an RFP with details and creativity.

- **Routinely monitor the competition's reviews.** Negative reviews about the competition are a sales opportunity! While you are not going to trash the competition to a meeting planner, you can subtly suggest that they take a look at Trip Advisor reviews of you and the competition in operational areas that are important to them. Be careful—your reviews in those areas had better be perfect! Set a Google alert for the hotels in your competitive set so that you are alerted every time there is a new post for one of them.

- **Participate in small group sites.** Many of the small group sites sort the hotels in the location requested by amenities that you either enter yourself or they are pulled from the GDS. Make sure that all of the amenities that would appeal to small social and corporate groups are listed clearly on your GDS description. Respond in the same timely fashion that you do to the RFP sites.

Do these habits replace the habits from last year—no, we still need to be proactively prospecting for new biz on the internet that fits the revenue management strategy. These 'new' habits open up new opportunities for prospects to reach you and your hotel—the playing field looks different but the game is still the same!

*(Jennings and Houghton, 2003)

The Habits of Highly Successful Hotel Salespeople Ramp Up for 2006!

The speed of sales has accelerated—no longer is it good enough to get back to a client within 24 hours. It is no longer good enough to get a proposal off to a client in two days. It is no longer good enough to blow off third party planners. It is no longer good enough to do sales this year the same way you did it last year!

"It's not the big that eat the small, it's the fast that eat the slow." (Jennings and Houghton, 2003). If you want to understand what the authors were talking about, think Google. While Microsoft was busy pounding Netscape into the ground, Google quietly developed and took ownership of Internet search until they rapidly became a verb, a wealthy verb.

Think Mapquest, when Rand McNally and AAA were still busy printing road maps and selling hard copies, little Mapquest made it easy and free to find your way to almost anywhere—online and instantly. By doing that it also became a verb. Have you heard anyone say "I am going to Rand McNally that"?

Think about what that really means, not in an abstract way but what it means to a hotel sales person every day, the habits they need to have in terms of developing new business and servicing existing accounts before the competitors get to them. Relationships are begun in the speed of an email and the sales process, if not dead, has been compressed and put on the life support of brief communications by email, voice mail, etc.

The article Habits of Highly Successful Hotel Salespeople that appeared in Hotel Online last September continues to be one of the most read articles in that publication every month. Those habits need to be ramped up for 2006 and 2007:

- **Web Enabled Cell Phones.** Blackberries, Treos whatever the brand make sure that every one of your salespeople has one. This is the phone number that should appear on every sales person's business card, electronic and hard copy. Highly successful hotel salespeople have their alerters set to be notified of new email and messages. They acknowledge the correspondence within minutes or hours. If they go on vacation to a deserted island, they make sure that a competent person is checking and responding like they would if they were there.

- **Research.** Prior to responding to an inquiry either from voice message or email the successful hotel sales person makes it a habit to log onto the prospect's web site to research more about them so that they can craft their response appropriately.
- **Masters of Communication.** It's not the college degree but the ability to use electronic communication to craft emails and deliver voice mails that get attention and appeal to the customer in such a way that the contact is eager to enter into a dialogue with them.
- **'Natural' Selection.** Not exactly Darwin but Darwinian in the way that the highly successful hotel sales person is able to develop, evaluate, pursue and book only that business that is aligned with the revenue management strategy. Not all inquiries and accounts will 'survive' the selection process—only those that meet the criteria necessary to maximize revenue for the hotel.
- **Natural Selection and Relationships.** The highly successful sales person understands that time is their most scarce and precious resource. Relationships have always been based upon mutual benefit. In the age of speed, relationships are built in 15 seconds and the ability to choose which relationships to nurture is critical—not only for proprietary accounts but also third party planners. The successful sales person doesn't wait to be contacted by a third party planner, they qualify and pursue those planners that represent accounts that have the potential to enhance the property's revenue management goals.
- **Google for New Business Development.** The successful hotel sales person does not wait for inquiries to come through the door; they aggressively seek accounts that fit the Revenue management strategy. They conduct Internet searches based

upon the DNA of accounts that they want to develop. They are not passive receptors but knowledgeable aggressors.

Are these the habits that describe your salespeople and the sales department? If they are, reward them based upon their production using a commission based model. It motivates the great ones, encourages the good ones and eliminates those whose skills might be better deployed in other areas.

Do you want your hotel sales department to be the diners or dinner? Remember "… it's the fast that eat the slow."

Habits of Highly Successful Hotel Salespeople

September 2005

Why do so many hotel salespeople fail or fail to live up to expectations? You know how it goes—a bright person interviews for the job, has a great smile, been 'successful' in other sales positions (always ask for numbers—don't take their word for it) and at the end of ninety days hasn't produced very much.

What is the 'tipping point'—that thing or series of things thing that makes one person successful and another less so? When both individuals have been trained in the same manner and have the same skill sets, why does one sales person excel and another languish in mediocrity? What makes the difference between 'average' and 'awesome'?

There are salespeople who come to the industry with no previous experience in hotels and are highly successful—outperforming their colleagues who may have been in hotel sales for many years. Usually but not always these are people who have come from commission sales of some sort. It is not necessarily the fact that other industries have better training programs (although many industries do a better and far more consistent job than much of the hotel industry), it is not just the sense of urgency that comes with having to create an income every month, it also has to do with the habits that they must develop in order to successfully pay the mortgage and eat.

This is not about being organized; I would rather have a top producer with a messy desk who is prioritized. This is not about time management, although that does play a part—it is about habits, daily disciplines that produce success. Like taking a shower, brushing your teeth, exercising, it is the habits that one forms about meeting goals, making calls, etc that distinguishes them from the others. I have known salespeople who were not the typical 'hot shots' succeed because they worked their plan every day without fail.

What are these habits that make 'awesome' instead of 'average'?

Daily Disciplines—Eating the Elephant One Bite at a Time. Successful salespeople take their goals, revenue, prospecting, calls etc. and break them down into monthly, weekly, daily activities. They have a good idea of their call to closing ratio, that is, how many calls, telephone or e-contacts, they need to make to close a contract. They know how many prospects they need to locate in a day and a week to meet their prospecting goals. They practice 'daily disciplines' every day.

Prioritize Activities. Not all activities, calls, traces, etc, are created equal. Prioritized salespeople call on those prospects most likely to produce revenue before they do the trace calls to say 'hello' to existing accounts—they prioritize their calls. They will cancel the Chamber of Commerce lunch if a prospective client wants to see them. They make time to prospect and pre-approach qualified prospects on the Internet AND they do that in non-prime sales time.

Think Revenue not Just Rooms. The successful sales person pays attention to the property's revenue management strategy and understands that the name of the game is revenue—not rooms. The revenue management strategy informs their prospecting activities. For example, in the SMERF market, the group of wine enthusiasts is more likely to pay the rate than the local scrap bookers club.

Whales and Tunas. Successful salespeople know that they need a mix of both large and small groups and accounts to meet their revenue goals and to balance out the group calendar. Some salespeople only want to pursue the big 'glamour' accounts. The problem with that is it takes much longer to land them than the smaller, less flashy, tunas. If the whale doesn't close within the timeframe of the sales person's goals, the sales person may not be there when the whale account eventually signs the contract.

'Intra-preneurs'. Successful salespeople treat their market or their territory like a business—their business. They function as intraprenuers within the organization. That makes them think creative and allows them to think out of the box in addressing issues within the organizations on their client's behalf.

Personal (Brutally Honest) SWOT Analysis. Successful salespeople evaluate their strengths in order to leverage it in to more business and maybe even a better position for themselves—don't forget the WIIFM factor! They are also honest about the areas where they could use some training and/or support and actively ask for it or seek out opportunities to get the training they need. They seek out opportunities in their market area and never underestimate the potential threats of competitors.

Sense of Urgency. Successful salespeople have a sense of urgency about working their plan because they know that if they fall too far behind it will be very difficult to catch up. They stay late when they have to and ask to leave early when they are caught up. Their sense of urgency is focused and directed not just a sense of urgency about activity, any activity. They choose their association memberships and functions carefully so that they only participate in those likely to be a source of business.

These are some of the habits that distinguish the 'awesome' sales person from the 'average' one—the super achiever from the ones that fail to meet expectations. There are sets of these habits that accrue to every management position in the hotel—the 'daily disciplines' that separate the great managers from the mediocre.

Hotel Sales Basics

Hotel Sales Basics Series—Some Things Never Change but Some Change Big Time

The following articles were written in response to a number of supposed 'hotel sales gurus' that said you need to make X number of cold calls to directories that begin with A and end in frustration. I had a Director of Sales say tome the first thing when I walked in the door for a consultation "I hate cold calls!" When I asked her why she pulled out the Chamber of Commerce Directory for a large metropolitan area and Said her General Manager told her to start cold calling everyone in the directory. No wonder she hated cold calls.

Sales basics are different from habits in that the basics of sales have to do with the processes by which we locate, qualify, present and close new business. These processes have changed substantially in a short period of time as I mentioned in the introduction.

As the planner, both transient and group, exerts more control over the buying process, prospecting becomes more complex. As well as Web 2.0 plays out, User Generated Content plays a greater role in that the prospect qualifies us through review sites, blogs and message boards, we are overcoming objections before we have a chance to present the product—but at least the objections are up front and we don't have to dig for them.

Online RFPs whether through RFP platforms or the hotel's web site are a great source of prospects that we may not have been able to find otherwise. This development however requires a new process in place to ensure that they are answered promptly, completely and creatively, if the hotel is to be set apart from the other hotels that the planner has sent RFPs to.

On the leisure social group side, more franchises and online RFP platforms exist for these groups to source information and request a bid from a hotel. On some of these sites, properties are sorted by amenities appropriate to the type of group rather than by price first. Many of these platforms also provide social networking sites where the groups can communicate about options and post pictures. The downside is that these groups are submitting RFPs through multiple sites and this can become confusing on the hotel side.

In light of these online RFP sites, it becomes even more important that hotel sales basics include best practices on email communication and that important information about the hotel such as meeting room diagrams, capacities and catering menus s are either digital to send to a prospect or available through the web site.

It becomes essential that information on all channels likely to be accessed by these groups prior to sending an RFP are complete and transparent, that is the same on all channels. For example, many times I log onto to a hotel web site and cannot locate how many guest rooms it has. If I were a meeting planner, I would move on and not necessarily contact the hotel because there are other options.

The things that don't change are the ability to make an effective presentation on why the planner should select the hotel—many times now it will be a virtual tour online versus a site visit. On a TravelMole survey 68% of meeting planners indicated that they would select a hotel based upon the information available on the internet and skip the site inspection.

Another thing that doesn't change is that salespeople still have to close the business—bring the buyer to the table and make the deal. Negotiation is also still a part of the process—this now occurs after the initial bid is made not prior to the bid.

Current accounts are still an under-utilized source of new business. We just never ask for the referral or about the other departments that plan hotel functions. Very few hotels completely penetrate an account but live in the delusion that they 'get all the business' from an account—rarely true!

There are important things to be gained from the first article and from the latest one which appears first.

Hotel Sales Basics for 2008—Some Things Change and Some Things Never Do!

As the end of 2008 nears, the industry is collectively waiting to exhale—unsure of where the economy is headed and what the impact will be on the industry. The research is contradictory. The 'chicken littles' are definitely sure that the sky is falling—the unfailing optimists who have reaped the benefits of the last five years are in denial that huge REVPAR gains and profits could be threatened.

The truth, hopefully will fall somewhere in the middle. Goldman Sachs "… is advising investors to shy away from the hotel business." Robert Mandelbaum with PKF published a scenario that indicated that "… if an economic recession were to occur in the United States during 2008—2009, it would result in a 6.1 percent decline in rooms revenue for the U.S. Lodging industry through 2010."

Smith Travel and American Express, on the other hand, believe that industry will remain healthy and life will be rosy for the foreseeable future. "… business travel demand will outpace capacity in 2008 and drive rate." As well, PKF predicts that the above scenario is just that and that realistically, REVPAR growth should continue to grow at 4.2% in 2008.

Hotels are now calling for basic sales training for their staffs that may be under additional pressure to perform if REVPAR slips. However with the complex relationship of the internet and travel industry and the implications of Web 2.0 impacts the basics of hotel sales.

With the increasing importance of User Generated Content including review sites, the client is taking more control over the sales process. Hotel sales basics now dictate that the processes include consideration of this change as it impacts group sales, both social and through meeting planners.

- **New Business Development—Three Primary Sources.**
- **Online RFPs**. Establish a process whereby someone in the sales office can filter the RFPs for those that are aligned with the revenue management and sales strategy and pass only those onto the sales appropriate sales person. The rest are sent a standard response requesting that the planner consider the hotel in the future.

- **New Business from Existing Accounts**. Most hotels have not fully drilled down into their best accounts for all potential new business. There is a process called Account Mapping so that the sales department has a 'map' of absolutely everyone at the account with the potential of booking transient, groups and catering business at the hotel. Each contact can then be qualified and assigned to the appropriate sales person with all of the information residing in a master file or database.
- **New Prospects**. What is the client DNA of your best accounts? Yes, I've said this before but most salespeople and departments still don't do it. Once the key characteristics of the property's best accounts by market segments and opportunity periods are identified, it is then a simple process to locate others like them and research them on the internet.
- **Qualifying**. How lucky are we that most of this can be done online and that many inquiries have already qualified the hotel online! Make sure that your online presentation is a good one so that when you make contact with the prospect, you can be more focused in the questions that you ask. Perhaps the most important qualifying question of all is "What things are going to 'tip' your decision in favor of one hotel versus the rest?"
- **Presenting**. Remember that in a TravelMole survey, 61% of planners indicated that they would make a hotel selection without conducting a personal site inspection. Develop online presentation skills when you take the planner to the web site—learn to paint 'word pictures'.
- **Negotiating**. Know what is negotiable and what isn't before you begin. Know at what point you will have to walk away. Negotiate on value—not price!
- **Overcoming Objections**. If you have qualified thoroughly there shouldn't be too many of these—you will have covered them in the negotiating process. Sometimes, people have hidden objections that have nothing to do with logic. Buying is often an emotional decision. Try to understand any 'hidden agenda' as you move through the process.
- **Closing**. This never changes—we still need to ask for the business! Close on something! Will you be using a direct bill or

a corporate credit card for the deposit? What is your decision making timeline for this event? When would you like me to follow up with you?

One of the big changes is that some of these steps with take place via email. Those communication skills and techniques need to be impeccable as much of the relationship building and maintenance will probably be done by email.

Back to the Basics? The Basics of Hotels Sales Have Changed!

The desperate effort by hotels to develop new business has resulted in a 'back to basics' movement. However, the basics of hotel sales have changed forever. The sheer size of most markets and technology dictate that sales becomes more efficient and effective. While the skill sets of selling techniques haven't changed, the way we locate and develop new business has to change.

Gone are the days when a sales person could walk the street and cold call everyone within a three or five-mile radius. Gone are the days when a cold phone call was returned and all it required was persistence. Gone are the days when the sheer volume of sales calls guaranteed success!

Even 'backyard marketing' requires new approaches. The sheer size of the 'backyards' of most urban and suburban sub-markets is too large for almost any hotel to physically or cold call on the telephone every potential business. I was working with one property and the sales person took me out to drive the market. A three-mile radius netted thousands of businesses due to the large number of industrial parks and very tall buildings. She said she was overwhelmed, where should she begin?

Another dilemma is the 'list'. Many salespeople are given lists of prospects in their market, trade show attendees from very large venues, etc. One sales person with whom I worked was given a two-inch thick state business directory by her GM. When she asked him where to start, his reply was to begin with 'A'. The total frustration that resulted from twenty cold calls per day only to be connected to voice mail and, in the event that she connected to a living human, to hear 'no' over and over again had resulted in 'burn out'.

The 'dead files' are another prospect source resorted to out of desperation. If these were such good leads, why aren't they in the active trace system to begin with? Sales departments are pulling out boxes or going through old filing cabinets of files that haven't been worked or followed up upon in years. Unfortunately, in many sales departments the task of calling the dead files often falls to the newest member of the team or worse, the sales assistant. These people are usually inadequately trained and, in the best-case scenario, given a list of questionss to ask and told to follow up with a packet of sales information. (Sales packets are another sacred cow that, in many cases, should become hamburger!)

If any of these lead sources sounds familiar, read on—there is a better way of dealing with each of these. But it is not the old 'basics', it is a new way slicing the lists and looking at the prospecting process.

- **Narrow down the 'backyard'—Know which industry sectors in your local market are out-performing the stock market.** Sales is not a job where you can just show up in the morning. Salespeople need to listen to the news, read the business sections of the newspaper—pay attention to what's going on in the business world surrounding them. The good ones do—the ones that don't won't be around long! Pay attention to the stock market. Those industry sectors whose stocks are rising have the money to conduct meetings and pay your rates. Look on the back page of the Money section in Monday's USA Today for a quick analysis of industry sectors. One industry sector doing EXTREMELY well right now is government subcontractors. Once you know which industries are performing well, do a search for those in your market. These are the ones you need to be calling on now!
- **Re-evaluate the lists—'slice' it to include only those who have the potential to give you business.** Instead of starting with 'A' obtain lists my market segments. Those of you who have access to Business Journal Top 100 lists, begin calling those that are in industries performing well—the sectors that you have gleaned from your research above. Log onto Switchboard. com for an industry sector in your city—see what comes up! Call those that are in relative proximity to your hotel or have

potential meetings. The Top 100 of industries that aren't doing well represent the best of a bad team! Remember, in the effort to save on travel budgets, those properties in 'drive' distance of the head office often have a good shot at landing the business.

- **Apply the same metrics to the 'dead' files**. If a 'dead' file hasn't given you business in two years or more, treat it as a new prospect for qualifying purposes. Before you call, check to see which industry sector it is in. You can do this by logging onto Hoovers.com or logging onto the company's web site. Don't just call and leave a message—deal with the file once and for all then retain it or dump it. In prioritizing the trace files, give first consideration to those that are doing well. This applies to associations serving the profitable industries sectors.

In this economy there are losers that are losing big but there are winners who are quietly making money out there. This applies to most market segments, corporate, the associations that support them and the SMERF markets. Government, that segment you loved to hate, is now a big winner in the room night generation category.

Smart prospecting takes more time, but is more profitable in the amount of time expended. Call activity becomes more productive and 'sales burn out' is less likely. Next month we will deal with effective ways to approach new business prospects, calling and leaving messages just doesn't cut it any more!

In this economy, and make no mistake, the recovery is likely to be delayed until 2004 at the earliest and even then will not return to the robust times of the mid-nineties. We in sales are going to have to refine our skills and the way we prospect and approach new business for the long term. The sales 'basics' have changed!

New Business Development—Separating the Awesome Hotel Salespeople from the Average

Web 2.0 has fundamentally changed the way hotel salespeople find, qualify and develop new business. No longer do hotel salespeople 'walk the street' and go from door to door to see if each business on every street within a specific radius has business for the hotel. We still need to penetrate the local market in order to maximize that opportunity but the internet has made this much easier.

Search has made it easier to find who is in the local market and qualify them on the internet. Search also makes it easier to locate new business that fits the revenue management strategies of the hotel based on client DNA.

Client DNA is more than a profile of potential clients, it also is a glimpse into who the people are that book the business. What does their 'dashboard' look like, how does the hotel get on their dashboard so when they are ready to buy, the hotel is there.

Customers want to buy but they don't want to be sold. If the 'beat the street' cold call is dead so is the cold phone call. No one misses either very much, especially the people that were cold called.

A recent survey on Mimegasite revealed that 54% of respondents were more likely to respond to an unsolicited email than to an unsolicited phone message. The email approach is about the prospect based on the research, not about he coffee makers or irons and boards!

It is those hotel salespeople who embrace and build creativity into these processes that will be awesome—the rest will remain average!

Client DNA—The Gold Standard For New Business Development

If you hate cold calls, the dilemma is how to find new business without using a list or a directory. What do you do to locate new clients that fit the revenue management strategy? Hint: Answering the phone and closing inquiries isn't it!

New Business Development or prospecting for business that fits the revenue management strategy is becoming more of an issue for hotel sales as demand softens. Anyone who receives the Smith Travel report for the US as a whole cannot help but notice that the demand index of occupancy began softening in the late third and fourth quarters of last year and has continued to do so Year to Date 2007.

While the REVPAR index has softened somewhat, it is only a matter of time before softening demand begins to exert downward pressure on rate growth in many markets. As the economy as whole is forecasted to experience a slower growth rate in 2007 and new supply in the pipeline comes online, there will be more pressure on hotel sales departments to develop new business.

What is Client DNA and how can it make the New Business Development process more efficient and effective? The DNA of a person determines what that person looks like and how they are 'wired'—the same principles apply to clients.

In the last election, both political parties developed the DNA profiles of their member and drilled it down into even specific precincts so that they could tailor their message to the preferences and habits of their members. For example, Republicans in some key precincts tended to buy their morning coffee from Dunkin Donuts or other fast food outlets while Democrats in the same precinct tended to go to Starbucks more often. Could I make this up!?

Just as the DNA profiles told the political parties about the buying habits of their members, so can client DNA give hotel salespeople information about the buying habits of potential clients and how they are wired. With this information, it is easier to locate potential new clients and craft a message that appeals to their DNA.

Developing client DNA by market segment and opportunity periods is a process. The following are the first steps:

- **The DNA of Existing Clients**. Who are they? Do they represent a particular industry or client group? Where does the booking originate geographically? What is the position of the person who booked the business? How did they locate the property? This is key, what was their 'tipping point' in selecting you and your hotel over the competition—that answer might surprise you!
- **Get Into their World**: How do they access information about hotels? What is the process they use in making lodging decisions? What associations or publications do they access to provide them tools to make judgments about the suitability of a property for a particular event? How did your property get on their 'radar screen'?
- **Communication**: How did the lead for this current client come to you? How did it originate—phone, email, referral? What is the client's preferred form of communication?
- **How Can You Plug Into Their World**? What info do they need from you to make a good decision? Hint: It is not a letter with bullet points of amenities like irons and boards, coffee makers, etc.! What will keep you on their radar screen so that you and your hotel are at the top of their mind when they are ready to 'buy', make a decision on their next function?

How do you find out this information? Ask the contacts at your existing good accounts the above questions—most people, if they like you and your hotel, are delighted to have the opportunity to talk about themselves. Delineating the DNA of current clients tells you how to locate and approach new accounts like them. Remember, in approaching prospective new clients, it's all about them not about coffee makers and irons and boards!

Hate Cold Calls?—Discover the New Paradigm of Hotel Sales

There is a huge difference in 'pushing' a product to new business prospects and 'pulling' or attracting new business to the hotel. The sales paradigm is shifting—not just in hotel sales but also in terms of the sales processes in most industries.

The 'cold call', in person or on the phone, is pretty much dead—no one misses it much. Anyone who is still using directories that begin with the letter A and end with total frustration know exactly what a waste of time it is. Many potentially talented hotel salespeople have been totally burned out by this method because the ROI is simply not there.

Potential clients check us out on the internet before they ever make contact with us. They receive industry newsletters and belong to organizations that discuss hotel experiences, both group and transient. People talk to other people in their positions in other organizations before they talk to you. These people are influencers who can make or break you.

Our potential clients also access the travel review sites. They know the difference between trivial problems and major issues—they are sophisticated enough to make judgments based upon the specifics in the online reviews. Do you know what the reviews say about your property?

How can you 'attract' a potential new business prospect to you and the hotel? It all begins with image, presence and reputation—both the hotel and the sales person.

- **The Web Site**. Put yourself in the client's perspective. Are you easy to find on the search engines, do you have a presence in key word searches? On the meetings and conventions page, is there a call to action? Does the list of key contacts have pictures and a brief profile of each sales person for each market segment? This is the age of communities, think "MySpace," where people are more comfortable contacting people they feel they know. For that matter, does the GM have a picture and profile? (The profiles should not include info on the person's family or the dog!)

- **Testimonials**. The positive reviews you get on guest comment cards or in post convention surveys should become an integral part of all marketing initiatives. Ask permission to use names and organizations—these become a third party reference that resonates with potential clients. These should be on the web site, electronic sales kits (you do have electronic sales kits and brochures, don't you?), one should appear on all correspondence, electronic and traditional as well as embedded in all presentations.

- **Become a Resource**. Become a resource to your clients in terms of the lodging industry and how trends in the lodging industry might affect them in terms of impacting their travel or meeting planning. Offer to talk about the local industry to meetings and associations of people in your market segment. This cannot be commercial for the hotel. Everyone belongs to the obvious meeting planner organizations, you know what they are and they are a wonderful resource. However, there's a lot of competition in those—seek out business organizations in your market segment and become a resource for them. Even if the planners themselves do not attend the meeting, let them know what you are doing and seek out others from their company or organization at the meeting.

- **Develop a Blog**. Create a community with your clients and potential clients by developing a monthly or quarterly blog. Salespeople are always looking for ways to stay in touch with their contacts without annoying them with 'Hi, how are you?' It's incredibly easy to do and you can send the link to all of your contacts when you add new stuff to the blog. Again, leave out the family and the dog!

- **Develop 'Attractive' Electronic Communication**. Cold calls may be dead but an attractive email approach with the WIIFM of your potential client in mind is alive and can be awesome. Give them value in the form of information that is useful to them and let them know that you have researched their business by approaching them with insightful references to their special requirements.

There are many other aspects to this 'attractive' business development paradigm and not enough space to detail it all in this article. Stay tuned for more. This is creative selling at its best—it's fun and a whole lot less frustrating than the directories that begin with A.

Partnership of Sales and Technology Using Tech Tools to "Sell" the Hotels

The hospitality industry has used innovation and imagination to manipulate and maximize tech applications for everything from revenue management to customer relationship management. Why then have we not given more thought to the creative uses of technology in the hotel sales process?

One answer is that while we have provided upgraded tech access to our guests, the sales department and administrative offices usually get hand-me-down hardware and sometimes are not even included in the high-speed Internet equation. In my consulting practice, I often go into the sales departments of relatively sophisticated hotels that are still on a manual system or have an automated contact management system that no one has ever trained them on because the sales staff has turned over several times since it was installed.

YIKES!

We need to put the same amount of creativity into applying technology to the sales function as we have in other functions of the industry—and it needs to be done at all levels of selling, especially at the property level! The use of technology in sales is then only limited by the imagination of the sales staff.

In my seminars, I often ask the participants how they are using their web site and virtual tours in the sales process. Those that have them indicate that they always refer clients or email a link to their site or virtual tour if one is posted. They are using the site as their primary fulfillment collateral and I recommend that. Save the money on the threefold color brochures and invest it in web site development.

However, pictures only tell, they don't sell. Pictures depict features not benefits.

I have often thought that hotel web sites should have tabs that are geared to the different market segments of a hotel. In this way, the copy and photography can be geared to the specific benefits of each market segment.

Current web sites are often like the old cover letters that salespeople used to use for every inquiry and follow-up. Those were the letters that "feature spewed" (pardon my language) by having a list of every conceivable feature in bullet points regardless of the type of client that it was addressed to.

The following are a few of the ways that hotel sales can use these tech tools to sell customers on the benefits of the hotel not just tell them about its features:

Voice Guided Virtual Tours.

Virtual tours are great tools. However, those that spin in a 360-degree view of a guest room make me a bit dizzy. As busy as most people are today, it is often difficult to get potential customers even from the same city to a hotel for a site inspection. However, rather than have the customer log onto the web site or take the virtual tour alone, why not establish a telephone appointment so that the client and the sales person can walk through the site while on the phone together? This allows the sales person to point out the features of the hotel that are true benefits to this customer and to sell the hotel's services. The sales person should prepare for this site presentation in the same way that they would for a "live" site inspection. The good news is that with a virtual tour, you don't have to pre-inspect the rooms and it usually doesn't cost you lunch.

In developing virtual tours on the web site, keep in mind that the average attention span of most people is relatively short. Pick the most representative digital photography for inclusion but limit your selections to those that will have the broadest appeal. I visited one hotel's site and they had eighty pictures posted—way too overwhelming for most site visitors. Granted it was a large hotel but when you have seen one boardroom, you've pretty much seen them all.

Bank of Digital Photography.

I learned this from one of my seminar participants from a resort area reservation service. The participant was the manager of the res office and she kept digital photography of all the properties and the destination on the hard drive of the computer, or a "bank" of digital photography. While on the phone with a potential guest, she would discover what "benefits" they were looking for in their destination and property selection. She would then ask them if they were online or if they could go online and she would email them photos of the features that fulfilled their expressed desires. She would then describe the picture in terms of the benefits to the potential guest. Need I tell you what her "capture" rate was for reservations?!

The "bank" of photography was the same as those used to build the web site. However, there were also some that were not used on the site. Most of the phone calls were from potential customers who had visited the site but had questions or concerns or simply wanted to speak to a live human versus making their reservations on-line. (Yes, there still are some of those around!)

Photography more often "sells" when it includes people using a feature of the hotel. For example, rather than simply having a photograph of the children's camp or playground, photos of children playing and having fun using these facilities sell the concept rather than just telling that the facility is there. Recall those stock photos of a hotel restaurant where people are sitting at the table staring at each other but not actually eating or drinking or appearing to have fun. The people in those photos were like the furniture.

The sales staff can use this photography in much the same way. Even if a planner has come for a "live" site, they often forget certain features. Many of them are coming to look at many hotels on the same trip. Depending upon the number of hotels that they tour, their memory will often place the bathroom of one hotel in another hotel's guest room. An emailed photo will refresh their memory or speak to question or concern. It can be a powerful tool to reinforce their initial impression and overcome a potential objection. For other groups, it can also provide an image of a benefit that a client requires in one situation that they didn't require in a previous meeting.

Photography of your destination and area attractions can assist you in making the sale and promoting off-site activities. This is more powerful than simply referring them to the local tourist organization's web site where they will also be exposed to other properties and perhaps rates.

Email Postcards.

Salespeople are always looking for creative ways to stay in touch with accounts. Email postcards can fill this requirement if kept fresh and not overused. I believe that everyone understands by now that unsolicited mailings in the form of letters never get opened. Postcards, on the other hand, receive a glance prior to being thrown away. You at least have a shot at gaining the recipients attention. Unsolicited attachments to emails are like mailings in envelopes. Busy people trying to manage their Inboxes most often delete them prior to opening. In addition, people are loath to open attachments that they are not expecting due to viruses.

An email postcard opens automatically. The visual appears in the recipients Inbox and is at least glanced at prior to deleting. This is an opportunity to gain the recipient's attention. Be very careful about not using this medium in a manner that could be considered "spam"—it should not be blasted to anyone who hasn't given "permission" to receive information about your hotel.

Let's differentiate between email "blasts" and approaching a potential new client. Email blasts to large number of recipients are extremely useful in informing past and potential customers about new developments or promotions at a property to those who have indicated a desire to receive them.

An email postcard can be a way to approach a prospect when telephone contact has failed as it does frequently. This is a tailored communication to one person versus a mass communication to many.

Email postcard templates are available on newer versions of Microsoft Publisher 2002/Deluxe Edition. They can be modified to contain your message or approach (remember to sell benefits to the prospect) and can contain a stock image or use an image from the bank of photography.

Microsoft Outlook and Outlook Express have a Stationery feature that allows you to customize designs and colors for emails. One of my seminar participants uses this to send attention-getting emails to clients and potential clients.

These are not to be used for email "blasts" but for customized communication to prospects and clients, especially when phone calls and regular emails get lost in the "chatter" of hotel solicitations. These postcards can set you apart from your competitors.

It's a tough market out there. Salespeople need creative tools to push the process forward. Those who are able to relate to their clients in a technologically sophisticated way exemplify that the property and the sales staff are prepared to offer their clients the services required in a high-speed environment.

Sales is the engine that drives revenue. Investing in tech tools and training salespeople to use them enables them to sell in such an environment. By ensuring that they have access to these tools, the property's exposure is enhanced.

I believe there ought to be a teaming of the sales department and the IT function to ensure that tech tools that are available to sell—not just tell. Imagine the power of those two creative forces—the possibilities are endless!

The New Realities of Hotel Sales—Focus on Revenue Generation

The issue of sales focus is not a very sexy topic but then January tends to be a month of focusing upon executing the plans made last year. The Marketing Plans are done (they are done, aren't they?) and now is the time to implement the ambitious goals laid out within them. None of this is going to happen unless and until the sales force is focused.

I walked into a hotel recently and asked the Director of Sales what the issues were that I could assist her with. She replied that one of them was Time Management. Over the course of the next few days I observed that she was easily distracted, had a very brief attention span and many of the other employees of the hotel would just drift into her office and "chat." She welcomed interruptions.

In another instance, I received a phone call from a client who asked me to keep an ear to the ground for a Director of Sales for one of his hotels. This client had just recently replaced this position so I inquired as to what happened. He replied that the DOS had resigned because she didn't want to be held accountable. They had just initiated a new reporting system.

There is a coaching client who welcomes the formulation of Action Plans and then has every "reason" not to execute them—the front desk needed help, he had so many meetings to attend, etc. You get the idea.

The issue here isn't really Time Management; it is the lack of focus. Sometimes it is a matter of organizing time but most often it is avoidance behavior. If they never have to execute the plan because of "other" distractions then they can't ever get rejected or fail.

My message to all of you to whom this behavior seems familiar is to get over it! One of the new realities of hotel sales is accountability. If salespeople are not prepared to operate in that environment then it is time for them to find a new career path. If salespeople are just waiting for the boom times to return when they weren't held accountable, move on, the "boom" times are not coming back any time soon.

Focus is not about getting organized—it is about being prioritized. The organization of bits of paper is not focus (and they said with computers we would become paperless—NOT). The organization of files or the folders in your Inbox are not focus. Focus is about deciding which things are priorities that generate new revenue and maintain business. Focus is about moving the ball down the field toward the goal every day!

There are things that salespeople and their managers can do to assist in developing a "focused" orientation:

Analyze Daily Activity

Force yourself to write down everything you do for a day and for how long. No cheating! Review it with management. I had a boss who asked me to do this once and it was very instructive for both of us. When we both analyzed it, it allowed each of us to understand where the other's priorities were and to align them so that we were working on the same issues. So often we do the things we think management wants us to do when they have different priorities.

Prioritize Activity

Calling existing clients to have a chat is not a priority—there is enough time at the end of the day to leave a message, send an email and say "hello." Messages and emails are wonderful things—they don't take long to write and they let the other person know you are thinking about them. Priorities are contracts, proposals, site inspections, finding new prospects—everything associated with revenue generation. Everything else can wait or be done by someone else!

Reduce or Eliminate Interruptions

I know a General Manager who, when her door is closed, attaches a pack of Post It notes to her door. Her staff knows not to interrupt her when the door is closed until after they have called the fire department! The staff writes down on the post-it note why they want to talk to her. She responds when she is done with what it is she is doing. The same applies to sales. Close the door; post a sign indicating that you are doing sales activity and that unless it is an emergency, please leave a note. You will be amazed at how few notes are left.

Prioritize the Task List

This assumes that most of you are using or have access to a contact management program. It could be ACT!, Outlook or any of the good hotel-specific programs on the market. They work only if you use them. (I check many of these with my clients and often find uncompleted activities from 2002.) You have the capability in many of these to assign a priority to each activity. Assign the highest priority to those that impact revenue generation. The rest can wait. Management, I would advise you to ask for the task list for the coming week as well as the activity report from the past week. This helps you and the sales staff to align the priorities of weekly sales activity.

True confessions time—my office is populated by stacks of paper that should go into files. Someone said to me once that I must be very organized. After I stifled a laugh, I replied no—I am prioritized. My priorities are my clients and the generation of revenue. My clients don't care about what my office looks like as long as I am serving them well. Your clients don't either—nor will management if you are generating revenue for the hotel.

Identifying the WIIFM Factor—The Essential of Hotel Sales Success

Hotel Sales Training that focuses on the sales process alone misses the point. There is no shortage of hotel salespeople that know the process. The pace of business is so fast that a salesperson that continues to go through the 'steps' often fails to hear buying signals.

Has anyone noticed in those Smith Travel reports that the demand side of the REVPAR equation is little bit delicate? Mark Woodruff of PKF points out the implications of that in a new study. "While the number of hotel rooms occupied will continue to grow at a 1.4 percent pace, the number of new accommodations is projected to increase by 2.0 percent in 2007. The net result is a forecast of a slight 0.6 percent decline in occupancy for the nation's largest lodging markets."

The implications of this is that hotel salespeople will be competing for business in 2007 and the trend that Mr. Woodruff outlines is expected to continue with Lodging Econometrics forecasting 119,426 new units in the pipeline for 2007 and 131,517 for 2008. Hotel salespeople will have to find new ways of differentiating themselves from the hundreds of other hotel salespeople vying for the same piece of business.

To a client the WIFFM (What's In It For Me) is the most important thing. When product and rate are relatively the same, a sales person who can zero in on what's 'personally' the most important thing to a customer is likely to make the sale. Hotel salespeople who can figure this out offer a powerful differentiation from the rest of the field.

In a recent seminar program, I asked the group please don't tell me that you are still sending those letters with bullet points that outline coffee makers, irons and boards, etc. An owner looked up at me and asked why not? The answer unfortunately is that nobody cares. The 'commoditiztion' of hotel rooms has made it so that those things are minimum expectations—everyone has those as well as TVs, beds, etc.

So in a world where the vast majority of hotels and rooms are relatively similar, what makes the difference? A hotel and a hotel sales person that can give the client what they want. Finding out what they want is the most important thing a sales person can do.

Salespeople are preoccupied with the 'pitch'—outlining every feature and every product that they can offer. When they are done, they pause as if waiting for the client to applaud. Even after the client gives them a buying signal that they are ready to buy, the sales person proceeds with the 'process' until they get the section on 'close'—nobody has time for that anymore.

From the first contact or approach, a sales person has to offer the client a benefit, a WIIFM, for engaging in a dialogue with them. People are just too busy to waste their time retuning a message, (they have way too many to return), or responding to an email unless there is something in it for them.

How do you find out the WIIFM?

- **Do the research**. Go online and check out the web site, go to Hoovers and check out their numbers. Is their revenue up or down, what does this mean for the contact person? Find out where they had this event last year—are you a comparable facility?
- **Ask your current clients in similar positions, "Why do you use our property".** If you are using the DNA model of new business development, you have clients similar to the one you want to approach. Existing accounts are a wealth of info about the hotel and why they use us—we just seldom ask them.
- **Put your self in their position**. Imagine that you are the prospect that you need to reach. What does the prospect's world look like? If you can't imagine your way into being them, find someone in a similar position and spend some time observing their world. What would be important if it were you?
- **When you make contact, ask them what is important in their hotel selection**. They will always say rate first because if they don't they are afraid that the sales person might overcharge them but that is usually not the deciding factor. Salespeople tend to get stuck in the 'qualifying' step asking things like number of rooms, arrival/departure pattern—important to us but we almost never ask them what is the most important thing to them.

Certain market segments are easier to figure out than others but one common response to this question is to make it easy. Staples isn't selling a bunch of those Easy Buttons by coincidence. We all are so busy we just want someone to make something easy.

The client wants a hotel that gets their reservations right, their rooming list correctly entered, and the catered function is on time, etc. Finally, they want accurate and timely billing—this all equates to EASY!

Go to Staples—buy a case of those EASY Buttons. Ship or take one to every new business prospect you are having difficulty closing and write a note that says, "This is what will happen when you book your next event at our hotel!"

Be prepared to deliver EASY!

The Tipping Point: Identifying The Touch Points In Hotel Sales

Identifying the touch points that tip a potential customer positively or negatively is an important issue in hotel sales training. Most sales training deals with all or some of the aspects of the sales process—ho, hum!

Experienced salespeople always express a certain 'been there—done that' in response or at best, say 'what a good refresher!'. So if they know it all why aren't they producing more is always the question.

In Malcolm Gladwells' book, *The Tipping Point*, it is emphasized that small things lead to big changes or a tipping point in which an situation or, in this case, a person or organization, is 'tipped' positively or negatively. If we apply the same principles to sales, we can identify those points of contact or 'touch points'. If we can identify them, then we can engineer or 'train' for them to ensure that they are positive.

Most of these should go without saying but it should never be taken for granted that even an experienced sales person is aware of and consistently executes these critical 'touch points' in a positive manner. 'Touch points' are behaviors that can be monitored and measured, which is more than most training ensures.

The measurement of these 'touch points', however, requires that we establish a new metric for reporting and observation. Instead of measuring only how much business was closed, from a training standpoint, we need to examine how the touch points were handled so we can reinforce the positive behavior. Equally important is to look at business that was lost and examine how the important touch points were handled that may have contributed to its failure to book.

Training to the desired behavior has a very definite practical application and forces a focus on the 'little things' that yield positive changes in 'tipping' the client in our favor. In a business environment of increased immediacy, it is critically important that each client contact or 'touch point' is maximized.

Do your salespeople have a Blackberry or a web enabled cell phone so that they can check and respond to emails while they are on the road? If the competition does, your salespeople may be too late. Remember, ***It's not the Big that Eat the Small—it's the Fast that Eat the Slow!"*** (Jennings & Haughton, 2003)

'Touch points' can be trained and some are more important than others. What are those touch points and what makes them important? A few are 'touched' upon below:

- **Initial contact.** Designate a response window as guidance for the sales person to return the communication. We always designate this but don't measure the execution. The window for responses is getting tighter and tighter and it is up to the sales person at the end of a conversation to commit to when the next action will take place.
- **The quality of the initial contact.** Getting it right the first time should not be tough. Whether the response is to be a phone call or an electronic communication, does the quality of that communication indicate that the sales person has listened and has crafted a response that reflects that?
- **Close on the next 'touch point'.** Let the client know when they can expect the response and how it will be delivered via email, phone call or snail mail (does anyone really put stuff in the mail anymore?).
- **"Do what you say you are going to do when you say you are going to do it".** How hard is this and how many people actually do it? It is a tough marketplace and it is indicative of how much this means when a client actually thanks a sales person for following up promptly.
- **Fast, fluent communication.** Relationships are built in five minutes—whether over the phone, email or in person. Quite frankly, a relationship doesn't mean much unless the sales person can get to the point and demonstrate the value of their product in terms that the client finds compelling.

All of the above rely on behaviors that can be trained for and measured. It is a matter of changing the paradigms with which we look at sales behavior and reporting—it is also a matter of whose salespeople will win in an increasing competitive market environment and 'tip' the client favorably toward your property.

Selling up! Taking Group Room Revenue to a New Level!

2006 is the year for hotels to maximize their revenue opportunities. Demand is high and new supply is low—new supply currently in the pipeline will begin entering the market in late '06 and '07. It is clearly a 'sellers' market this year! Hotel sales departments clearly have an opportunity!

Hotels that may have grown a bit 'tired' in the lean years are now investing in capital improvements and extensive renovations as there is finally the cash to do this and it is imperative to remain competitive at the desired higher rate tier. Investors and owners, however, want to see the return on this investment.

In recent conversations with contacts in the industry, there are mixed messages. On one hand, meeting and travel planners are concerned that rates are going through the roof and deals are getting tough to negotiate. On the other hand, Vice Presidents and Directors of Sales, express concern that group room rates are not increasing at the same pace as rates from other channels.

There are no easy answers but answers nevertheless. In both camps, the players need to make some tough adjustments. From the meeting planners perspective there is tremendous pressure to keep travel budgets at least level with last year,(see Hotels Are in the Drivers Seat!, Hotel Online, November 2005).

If it is the year that 'Hotels Are in the Drivers Seat', why do so many salespeople have such a tough time asking for and getting the rate? Often it is a matter of mind set versus purely a skill set issue. There are a few factors that play into this:

- **Length of Tenure**. How long have the salespeople been at the property? If they have been through the tough times, they may be stuck in the recession mentality. If they were responsible for selling a 'tired' property that has been recently renovated, the reality about what the new product is worth may not have set in. What both need to realize is that it was never ALL ABOUT THE RATE anyway! As a wise man once said, if rate was the only issue, the economy hotel products would be full every night and they aren't!

- **Who signs the paycheck?** Salespeople often have a great need to be liked. They have a long-standing relationship with a client that they want to keep happy even as that client is hammering them on the rate. Never walk into a negotiation that you are not prepared to walk away from. Salespeople forget that it is the hotel that signs the check and if the client is inflexible, given the changed circumstances of supply and demand, they need to stand their ground and present the value of the product. What can you buy today that you paid the same price for last year?

- **Breaking Up is Hard to Do!** Not every client who used the property in the past when times were leaner or before the renovation is going to make the cut. In order to drive the revenue, it is often necessary to change the client mix. Be willing to let go of accounts that cling stubbornly to their old rate. Refer them to another property that can meet their rate demands.

- **Mining for Higher Rated Business**. This is also called prospecting and New Business Development. Most salespeople don't have time to prospect because there is *soooo* much to do servicing existing accounts (see above!), communicating with the Front Desk, Food and Beverage, attending meetings, etc. It's a new world out there—those who are able to replace lower rated accounts with new higher rated business will win the 'Task'! Those who won't or don't'—how many of you watch "The Apprentice?"

- **Change the Compensation or Incentive Structure**. I really hate to repeat myself but there is evidence that many hotels are listening and modifying their compensation program to reflect productivity. When the economy is good and everyone makes budget by answering the phone, it is very easy to be complacent. It is the industry standard of salary plus bonus tied to property revenues not individual productivity that has kept the hospitality industry from attracting the best and brightest salespeople in the past.

Hotel salespeople, and I love them, need to realize that they are in the Drivers Seat and what that means to them. Go ahead—take a risk, ask for a higher rate! Try not to look surprised when you get it!

Market Trends

Introduction

The hotel industry is cyclical—dependent to a large extent on the condition of the economy. As the economy fluctuates so does the hotel industry. Both the economy and the hotel industry have been so strong for the last five years and many people tend to forget what down cycles look like.

In 2008, we may again see this relationship between the hotel industry and the economy take a turn downward. The research is conflicting as to how far the economy may turn—a dip or a full blown recession where GDP actually declines.

Strategies in terms of rates and demand management fluctuate with the economy. Travel is a controllable expense to corporations and the associations that support them. Leisure travel and SMERFE are based upon disposable income. When people have less disposable income these market segments suffer.

I can hear it now—the articles on rate strategies actually suggest negotiating lower rates when the rooms are going to go empty. This has not been the case in most markets for so long but if a dramatic downturn occurs, they may be useful reading.

The hotel industry has done an excellent job of managing revenue and rates in the recent past. Because the revenue management tools are more sophisticated than they were the last time there was an economic softening, the result on rates may not be as severe but make no mistake—if demand declines it will only be a matter of time before there is downward pressure on rates.

The Contingency Hotel Sales and Marketing Plan—Hope for the Best, Plan for the Worst

In this economic climate, there are hotels that will continue to generate revenue and those that will generate excuses. What will be the difference—those hotels that develop contingency plans with measurable 'triggers' versus those that sit by and watch the economy take its toll on their revenue base.

Most hotels' sales and marketing plans were completed prior to the accelerated downturn of Q4 last year. "The Central Bank said it now sees the economy growing at a rate between1.3% to 2% this year, down from its previous forecast from October of growth between 1.8% and 2.5% for 2008." (CNN, 02/20/08).

If that wasn't bad enough it also predicts that "… it expects the unemployment rate for the year to be between 5.2% and 5.3%, up from the 4.8 % to 4.9% range previously given." Why is this important? When unemployment begins to be an issue combined with the crisis in the housing market and decreasing home values, disposable income drops and travel becomes more constrained.

Corporations are examining their travel polices to reduce the number and/or size of meetings and reducing unnecessary travel. Smith Travels' latest statistics for the week of February 9 for the entire US market reflect a decrease in demand of 4% while ADRs increased by 4.8% resulting in a REVPAR increase of .8%

Even Wendy's rolled out its contingency plan to counteract more cost conscious consumers by increasing its dollar menu and adding low cost wraps. What are you doing to insulate yourself from economic downturns in your key market segments?

If you have a hotel in a market that is doing well, don't become complacent. There is normally a lag time before the impact of declining economic indices is felt. Perhaps the hotel's market will remain insulated from the declining economic indicators—tech stocks and related industries are in a market sector that's thriving. However, better to have a plan in place with actionable triggers and not need it than not to have one in place if the market goes soft.

What are the elements of a sales and marketing contingency plan?

- **Monitor all market segments that could be impacted.** RSS feeds give you instant up to date access to economic news. For example, the Sharper Image filed for Chapter 11 Bankruptcy the day I am writing this newsletter. GMAC announced an hour ago that they will close 15 of their 20 North American offices an hour ago. How are you staying on top of developments at your large accounts?
- **Develop a plan on how to counteract similar situations with your top accounts.** Sharper Image filing Chapter 11—who thought that would happen? Don't wait for it to happen—develop a plan with actionable steps on how you would counter the loss or cutbacks in primary accounts through other sales and marketing initiatives. For example, if a major account drops 5% (the measurable 'trigger') in production, which smaller higher rated accounts that may have been displaced by the discounted RFPS can you pursue?
- **Check in with groups on the books**. For both corporate and SMERFE groups, check in and see how their attendance is shaping up. Don't wait for them to call you with room block reductions and/or cancellations. Develop an action plan to replace lost revenue on a short term basis if necessary—ecommerce initiatives offer excellent opportunities to do this.
- **Every contingency plan needs measurable 'triggers'.** This means that if a large account reduces production by X%, you will pull the trigger on a plan to replace it. The same with groups, if a group of X number of rooms cancels, have an ecommerce plan in place ready to go to replace the revenue and rooms.
- **Treat every inquiry and RFP like gold**. Inquiries are an opportunity to have an introduction to an organization or company hat you may not have known about otherwise. The inquiry isn't just about the event that they are inquiring for, it is an opportunity to qualify an account for additional business.
- **Resist the urge to cut the training budget.** This economic downturn has come on relatively suddenly after a prolonged period of relative prosperity. This means that you may have

salespeople that have only known the good times and may not have the skill sets to sell effectively for the difficult times. Tom Peters wrote that the average company in North America only spends 26 hours on training per year per employee and that it is difficult to develop champions on that training schedule. Do you think Tiger Woods only practices 26 hours a year?

The economic ugliness is expected to linger until sometime in 2009 according to the Bloomberg report. Take the steps to protect your revenue base and enable contingency strategies to thrive in a down economy. Heroes are developed in tough times not in good times— generate revenue not excuses!

Contingency Hotel Revenue Management Strategies—"I Will not Cut Prices"

"Everyone repeat after me: "I will not cut prices nor panic sell because it does not stimulate incremental demand and only serves to drive down prices." (Jeff Weinstein, Editor, Hotels Magazine, February 08) Jeff has given us the mantra that all GMs, Revenue Managers and Directors of Sales should repeat every morning.

While most analysts have continued to be bullish on revenue increases of at least 4% in 2008, that was before the employment numbers began to slide. PKF, in its January research article indicated that although the industry was well positioned to weather the storm, there was one caveat. "What will keep the economy buoyant, as well as the lodging industry, is the continued growth in employment. Historically, we have seen a strong correlation between changes in employment and lodging demand," Woodworth observed. Unfortunately, the assumption of a continuing employment growth turned out to be short lived as the latest two government indicators showed significantly slippage in this area.

The erosion in the economy has been relatively rapid. A survey of over 1600 meeting planners indicated that for only 37% of them were their meeting plans for 08 were unaffected by the economy. (MeetingNews on MiMegasite February 26, 2008)

Okay, disposable income upon which leisure travel is dependent is shaky, the continuing credit crunch is impacting corporate travel and now the meetings market, what is a revenue manager to do to stop the bleeding and stimulate demand if not cut rate?

- **Monitor Changes to Market Segment Activity Daily.** This should go without saying but many daily flash reports do not carry lines that compare daily activity year over year by market segment or month over month or YTD by market segment.

50

Reports that include percentages of occupancy by market segment are a graphic way to detect downturns. This is an 'early warning' signal that will allow you to take action before the slippage becomes worse.

- **Manipulate the Rate Structure—don't lower it!** Closely monitor inventory and rate on the OTAs. Open discounts to more room types during periods of low demand. Participate in promotions with the OTAs until you reach the goals of the promotion. Close inventory to lower rated rooms when demand warrants it. Train the reservations staff to close each reservation by skillfully offering room type options at different price points if that's what it takes to convert the call.

- **Evaluate Channel Distribution.** When the revenue management strategy was first developed last fall, what were some of the distribution channels that were not included due to high commissions, relatively low production, etc? A high commission on some revenue may be better than no commission on unsold rooms. Were the Opaque channels abandoned as requiring too deep a discount? A discount on an opaque channel is not a lower rate structure but a way to expose inventory to markets that you may not have exposed the hotel to in the past. In both of these scenarios, you control the inventory.

- **Dynamic Packaging.** Packaging options on the hotel website, distribution channels and channels such as TravelZoo provide an opportunity to expose your hotel, generate incremental revenue and 'disguise' the rate within the package. Packaging on the hotel's web site is the cheapest and easiest way to generate incremental business but you have to drive your customers and potential customers to the site through effective SEO (Search Engine Optimization) and CRM initiatives.

- **Monitor the Hotel's Online Presence.** Especially in difficult times it I more imperative than ever to monitor the hotel's online presence. Pet peeve, make sure that the links work everywhere you are listed. I logged onto a CVB site recently and four of the seven hotels whose links I clicked didn't work. You can't have an online presence unless you are 'present'. There are tools that can assist you in this that can make this process easy and give you the info to make good decisions. The Avalon Buzz Report among others makes monitoring your online presence and that of the competition easy. These reports can also expose opportunities to fill gaps in demand with ecommerce initiatives.

- **Correct Deficiencies.** If your hotel presence online monitoring tool uncovers areas where you are not in rate parity, correct immediately. As well, there may be some links on sites that were enabled years ago that no one was aware of and are therefore unattended. These can have erroneous information and rates. I discovered this with a simple search for an independent hotel client. The hotel was offering an NFL special on an obscure site that no one at the property was aware of.
- **Respond to Critical Online Reviews.** Respond with a measured response to any online review as to how the deficiency has been corrected and or how a situation surrounding a less than optimal guest experience occurred. Ensure that there are no areas of the hotel that you would not like to see in pictures or videos posted on TripAdvisor. One client took the response thing to a whole new level and even responded to positive reviews with a Thank You response!

Diligence and creativity are the hallmarks of crafting a contingency revenue management strategy and for many of you the time to implement a contingency plan is here. I suggest one more thing to implement at your stand up meeting each morning with the GM and DOS. Prior to analyzing the numbers and starting the day, repeat Jeff Weinstein's mantra, in unison—"I will not cut prices!"

Playing The Rate Game—Positioning, Positioning, Positioning

If the three important factors in real estate are location, location, location, the big three in playing the rate game are positioning, positioning, positioning!

The last edition of this newsletter aroused vigorous debate via email, at a seminar that I presented for the Wisconsin Innkeepers Association annual meeting and at a corporate seminar that I recently conducted. Let me say it one more time, I am not advocating a wholesale reduction of the rate structure of any hotel. What I am advocating is the positioning of the rate structure vis-a-vis product and rate category and the discounting of rates to fill opportunity periods in the form of special promotional rates for certain time periods.

Selective discounting has to be well targeted by market segment or specific client profiles that can address those opportunity periods. This principle works equally well for corporate based hotels as well as resorts.

Let's look at some specific examples. A corporate hotel is running in the mid sixty-percentile midweek. This is significantly lower than in previous years and their midweek prime occupancy period is running one day shorter than in the past. They now are running 60-65% Tuesday and Wednesday nights while Mondays and Thursdays have fallen to approximately 50%. For simplicity's sake, let's say that this is a 100-room hotel, which means that on any given night, they have between 35 and 50 rooms to sell. There is a highway construction project in the area and their competition for that business is a limited service property across the street.

In this situation (an actual one) the General Manager was smart enough to realize that an additional 15 rooms for five nights a week was worth lowering his rate to $46 ONLY for this specific group. He included a coupon for a $4 discount on a full hot breakfast, something that he does for all of his government accounts (a segment that has increased by 15% due to this) and successfully landed the business even though his competitor was offering a rate $2 cheaper.

Say what you will about lowering rates but this hotel is running ahead of last year in revenue, market share penetration and REVPAR in a market where all of these indices are declining among the competitive set.

Let's look at another example, a resort situation. This property is newly renovated and presents well. However, the statistics indicate that their Occupancy and REVPAR have been declining in inverse proportion to their rate. In addition, an aggressive competitor is 'dogging' their rate, that is, the competitor is entering into the reservation system a promotional rate that is $10 to $30 less based on opportunity periods. Once the GM realized this, he met and in some periods reduced his promotional rate to be slightly lower than theirs. He is only offering so many rooms at this rate so he can build his occupancy and rate structure. This is called yield management, an art that has been lost of late. When this GM analyzed his actual fill nights in high season, he realized that there was some opportunity there as well, i.e., he was not as full as he thought at mid-week during high season. The hotel is now actively targeting a lower rated market segment; skiers at colleges and universities within drive distance, who have the potential to use the resort during this period. The rate is very discounted rate and they are promoting it directly to the institutions student unions and through student newspapers. Creative thinking out of the box!

I challenge you to do the following:

- **Make sure that your rate is positioned properly** against the competition by shopping their reservation system and analyzing their positioning on the electronic distribution channels. They may be undercutting you without your even knowing about it.
- **Analyze your data** for the past two years. In many ways 2001 was not representative, especially Q4. Find out how many 'fill nights' you actually had versus what you think you had.
- **Use this data to identify opportunity periods** where selective discounting can benefit the hotel.

- **Think creatively out of the box**. Develop a strategy with your sales department and reservations to 'fight back' and target those market segments that can fill your opportunity periods
- **Be willing to take risks**. Not every idea will work or work immediately. If you are cost-analyzing your promotions, you won't be out of pocket too badly if the first idea doesn't produce as well as you thought. Move onto the next one.

These are examples of rate positioning and selective discounting to fill rooms that would otherwise be left empty. Stubbornly holding on to a rate structure or rate because 'the product is worth it' will leave you with declining revenues, REVPAR and market share. Your product is only worth what people are willing to pay for it at any given time.

The Rate Game—Playing to Win

Confusion abounds in regard to where the rates should be. There is still a segment of the hotel population that is in denial and wants to keep rates at their 2000 level because "the product is worth it." Sales is frustrated that they are losing business to other hotels that are slashing rates in a bid to increase occupancy and getting grief from above because they can't "sell the rate." Neither stubbornly maintaining rates nor 'slashing' works in the current economic climate.

The nature of the rate game has changed. In the above scenario which side is playing the playing the game to win? Neither. If this were a gaming table in Las Vegas, both sides would lose their shirts.

Make no mistake, in the first scenario the product is only worth what someone is wiling to pay. If fewer people are willing to pay, market share declines and the REVPAR and Yield Indices are out of balance. In the second scenario, slashing rates may build market share penetration but REVPAR and Yield will decline to unacceptable levels.

I would submit that there is a smarter way to play this game so that both sides have a win-win and ultimately the hotel wins. However, only certain players can play this game.

The first qualification is that you had to have enjoyed market share above 100% until at least Q4 2001 and your current published rates are positioned well against the competition in your product category. All others shouldn't come to this gaming table until they have at least established the second qualification above.

Leave the published rate structure alone. You have probably already noticed a sharp decline in rack, corporate and other programs tied to rack rate as well as a sharp increase in the discount market segments. Somewhere in the middle is the 'value rate.' This is the rate that the middle 50% of your customers are paying, those that have negotiated rates or LNRs, large group rates, etc. The increase in rooms in the discount segment should offset the loss in rack segments. It is the average rate paid by your locally negotiated accounts that is probably your 'value rate' in the market. By 'value rate', I mean the rate that is considered good value by those in your local market with the potential to give you business and those that call the hotel directly rather than Central Reservations. This should become your 'sell' rate across the front desk for walk-ins and reservations.

Discount everything else like crazy! Actively seek out and aggressively bid on tours, one-time groups like construction crews and large groups from accounts that you know are bidding out meetings or groups. Selectively trade rate for volume in Q4 2002 and Q1 2003. This takes a certain amount of skill on the part of the sales person.

Here are some of the steps to follow:

- **Prospect all those files that you previously rejected because the rate was too low.**
- **Keep your eye on your competitor's parking lot for tour buses and company vehicles**. Know who is using your competition at what rate—if you don't know call and shop them.
- **Get a clear understanding of the lowest rate you can quote and the guidelines**. You want to be able to close on the first call—don't be in the position of having to check and call back. If you can pique the prospect's interest you need to be able to act on that opportunity.
- **Call them and grovel**—indicate that you are offering substantial discounts on a limited basis.
- **The first person to quote a rate loses**! Ask them what rate they are looking for, their budget for this project, what they are currently receiving elsewhere and what it would take to get their business. You may not be able to meet or beat the rate but at least you know what the ballpark looks like and you can value-add to make your slightly higher rate more attractive.

This strategy works if you are projecting few or no 'fill nights' in the fourth and first quarter. You have inventory to sell. Anything that you sell in these circumstances is incremental.

The benefits to the hotel include increased market share, incremental revenue and the ability to retain staff during a down period. This is playing the Rate Game to win!

Make no mistake about it—those properties that maintain or increase market share in these economic times will be the ones well positioned to move the rate when the economy begins to turn upward!

Is the Party Over? The Challenge of Decreasing Demand

Is the party over? Has the hotel industry been lulled into becoming 'fat, dumb and happy' after the stunning REVPAR growth of the last 2+ years? Has the industry peaked and is now on the downside of the curve?

Smith Travel reports that nationwide demand was virtually flat this summer and began to decline by 4% or more in the last two weeks of September. Mark Woodworth with PKF forecasts that for full service hotels nationwide in 2007 demand will increase by only .04%, ADR by 2.5% and REVPAR by only 2.9% versus a forecasted 9.5% increase for 2006.

For the top 51 markets in the US, those predicted to experience the most growth are both in New Jersey, Newark and Edison and they will post gains in REVPAR of 6.2% and 5.3% respectively. At the bottom of the list is the market of Miami, expected to decline in REVPAR by 6.5%.

The question is how many hotel budgets were conceived in the haze of the 'irrational exuberance' of the past two years, to quote Alan Greenspan? Those that were based on historical numbers and not industry forecasts will lean on their sales departments to fill in the gap between the budget and reality.

In the past several years, the role and function of the sales department has changed substantially in some hotels. In many hotels (but certainly not yours!) sales has been relegated to the role of 'order takers' and bookers of "SMERF" groups to fill in the slow times as burgeoning demand was beating down the door to get in most of the time. Having seen this happen in other periods of peak demand, this is not surprising.

As the cycle turns downward, the expectation is that sales will have the right staff and the right skills to generate demand that hasn't been pursued for several years. What can management do to gear up the sales pipeline in a hurry to counter balance the decline in transient demand?

- **Evaluate the current staff.** Do you have the right people who are up for the task? If management has been just hiring warm bodies to answer the phones, you may need to obtain a professional and objective evaluation and perhaps redeploy some of them to other areas in order to make room for professional salespeople with a track record that can deliver the business. Will good salespeople or people with the right stuff be more expensive—probably!
- **Provide a targeted training and support program.** Don't just throw them into one generic seminar and expect that will do the trick for the entire year. The revenue management and sales strategies need to operate in concert and that requires that specific training and ongoing support so that they can develop new business targeted to the opportunity periods of the property. The SMERF segment alone won't cut it anymore.
- **Rebuild relationships.** In the past several years when demand was high, many marginal client relationships may have been neglected or 'blown off'. Now, the hotel may need these clients. Sucking it in and retrieving an account that has been intentionally neglected requires the skills of a true sale professional. (See point one above).
- **Develop a targeted distribution strategy.** There are new distribution options evolving and coming to market all the time that can help fill your rooms. Can you name more than the obvious ones that you have grudgingly used in the past? Evaluate the cost of promotions on these and the GDS against the incremental revenue they can provide.
- **Develop a Customer Relationship Management Program.** When you mention CRM to most hotel managers they begin to twitch because they either don't understand it or mistakenly think that all the options are expensive. There are even CRM options that you can put together yourself at very little cost. The cost of retaining existing guests is far lower than acquiring new ones.

These are a few things you can do to protect your property's revenue from a slowing economy but do them NOW! Don't wait until senior management or ownership is on your back to put these pieces in place. If the forecasts are wrong, you will have contingency strategies in place—if they are right, you will maintain share instead of trying to find quick fixes to steal share!

REVENUE MANAGEMENT—
The Strategies that Guide the Hotels Revenue Maximization

Hotel revenue keeps morphing as a discipline—becoming more complex as technology and online tools change. The Web 2.0 phenom has given rise to a concept called the hotel's online presence. This means every place that the hotel is present online in addition to the web site it includes reviews on the reviews sites, entries on blogs and forums as well as any photos or videos that may have been uploaded to any review or social media site.

The revenue manager's job is to monitor the hotel's online presence and optimally, that of its competitors. There are many tools with varying degrees of complexity on the market that provide a convenient dashboard that the RM can use to monitor the hotel's online presence.

Revenue management is the ultimate team sport. It is the revenue manager's function to provide the data to sales, the GM and sometimes others involved in the Revenue Management decisions. The RM has the responsibility to make recommendations to the rest of the revenue management committee and many have now taken over the transient consortia RFP function bidding and monitoring function.

Revenue Managers no longer only monitor demand and inventory but are responsible for influencing and generating revenue. It is the revenue manager that maintains the relationship with the market managers at the OTAs. In consultation with the revenue management committee it is the revenue manger that opens and closes rates and inventory on all channels.

The revenue manager is now an executive committee member and hotel companies have Vice Presidents of revenue management. In the not so distant future, revenue management will become a path to the President's and CEO's offices.

Habits of Highly Successful Revenue Managers Ramped up for 2008!

Life used to be relatively simple for hotel revenue managers—the daily disciplines were relatively straightforward—check the reports, balance the inventory, check the channel contributions, review fences and hurdles, etc., etc. In most hotels, the process has become more complex and the disciplines are multiplying almost exponentially due to the complexity prompted by the impact of Web 2.0 on the competitive hotel environment.

As if that were not enough, the new PKF econometrics model that estimated the impact on the industry of a potential economic recession was released this past week. "A recently released analysis by PKF Hospitality Research (PKF-HR) found that if an economic recession were to occur in the United States during 2008—2009, it would result in a 6.1 percent decline in rooms revenue for the U.S. lodging industry through 2010."

Both of these developments have intensified the 'habits' of revenue managers at the property level and beyond. In many properties the revenue manger is also the sharing the ecommerce role with sales and marketing. Independent hotels that often don't have resources available to them that some of their franchise competitors do, will have to stay on the cutting edge of both of these developments if they are to be successful.

While a recession may or may not happen, the competitive impact of user generated content or Web 2.0 on the hotel industry is a definite reality that is not going away. If the hotel does not have an ecommerce manager or a large sales department, the monitoring function of the hotel's online presence and ecommerce initiatives often falls to the revenue manager.

Highly successful revenue mangers are motivated by the challenges of both opportunities. Some of the new Habits of those Highly Successful Revenue Managers are:

- **Monitoring the hotel's online presence**. User generated reviews sites are multiplying rapidly. As a recent survey showed, the reviews play a larger role in the decision making process for the consumer than price (Yahoo Travel Survey 08/07). How the hotel is presenting to the travel community through the various sites upon which it appears and is reviewed is critical. There are third party monitoring programs at various price points and levels of complexity that can assist in this but properties with small budgets can set Google alerts for the property name so that every time something is posted on the internet about the hotel, it is directed to the Revenue Manager's Inbox. This may be the 'rawest' of data but it beats no data at all!

- **Monitoring all links to the property**. A recent study attempted to direct an online RFP through various property web sites and found that nearly half of the links on the property web site for RFPs either didn't work or were directed to an email address that was no longer valid. Links on various directories on which the property is listed may also be old and directed to email addresses that are no longer valid—this was a finding in recent research for a client. It would be nice to believe that the web master would check the links on the web site but the reality is that it is not their job. People leave the company but there is no audit of everywhere that links to their email appearing in the hotel's link strategy.

- **Managing the relationships with the OTAs**. Expedia estimates that for every dollar spent on this web site there is another dollar spent on the hotel's web site or other direct contact such as phone. The implication of this is that the OTAs have now become hotel 'search engines' used by consumers to research the hotel options at their destinations. Couple this with the fact that the OTAs now also have increasingly robust review functionality, and their influence is growing. This makes those Merchant Agreement agreements for exposure and page placement even more important. However, merchant agreements proliferate in some markets. This may prompt the OTAs to establish levels of Merchant Agreements such as Gold, Silver or Bronze or some variation, in order to manage the increasing demand for Merchant Agreements. It makes it even more important to establish and maintain close relationships with the Market Managers, ensure rate parity and explore opportunities for greater exposure though packages, for example.

- **Contingency Revenue Management Strategy**. No one, not even PKF, can predict with any certainty the implications for the hotel industry of the current 'nervous' economic climate . Therefore, smart Revenue Managers and Directors of Sales, for that matter, will take the time to develop contingency plans in case of the worst possible case scenario mentioned in the PKF study earlier. The contingency plan should include market specific hotel intelligence as well as micro economic information with regard to how vulnerable the local market is to downturns in the various sectors of the national economy. The contingency plan would include certain developments that would 'trigger' pre-determined adjustments in the RM strategy. For example, if a current RFP account announces production cutbacks or layoffs at a facility in the local market, this triggers certain actions in the allocation of inventory and rates given the anticipated reduction in that account's room night production at the hotel. It is far better to have a contingency plan that is not needed than to need an alternate strategy and have to develop it at the last minute when it may be too late.

The habits of highly successful revenue managers have become more complex in just a short period of time. The truly good RMs will embrace the change—those who fail to adapt to change risk the fate of all who fail to 'read' changes in the environment and adapt. Anyone remember the dinosaurs?

Five Revenue Management Tactics for Independent Hotels

It's not the big that eat the small, it's the fast that eat the slow"
(Jennings & Houghton, 2005).

For independent hotels that's good news. Independent hotels and resorts may not have all of the resources available to them that their franchised counterparts do but they have the advantage of greater flexibility—independents can gear up or down in a flash!

There are some challenges ahead this summer that need to be monitored for their impact in specific markets. PriceWaterhouseCoopers has predicted that 2007 summer will be a record year for the number of occupied hotel rooms; however, "… The summer occupancy in 2007 is forecast to be slightly lower than 2006, 69.6 percent, … and approximately a percentage point below the 70.2 percent occupancy in 2006."

In addition the study goes on to say that the price of gasoline is finally taking a toll American's travel habits. "… The price of gasoline will result in approximately 8,000 fewer occupied rooms per night, or 0.2 occupancy points." An 8,000-room decline spread nationwide does not appear to be a lot but for hotels that operate in markets that are seeing significant new supply, the impact on the market will be more profound.

As the demand number becomes more delicate, it was inevitable that "there is also emerging price resistance following hotel average daily rate increases of 5.5 percent and 7.1 percent in 2005 and 2006."

There are five basic revenue management tactics that independents can implement to be nimble and responsive in the face of changing demand and rate patterns:

> **1. Check Pricing Strategy Against Last Year's History.** How many fill nights on what days of the week in the month did you have last year? Are rates adjusted accordingly based on those demand patterns as well as this year's groups, special events, etc? Do you have the nerve to be the last to fill at the highest rate?

2. **Close Discounts.** This may be a no-brainer for some but many hotels leave their 10% discounts open such as AARP and AAA. The rationale is that it is only 10%—how much is 10% on a rate of $100 times the number of rooms you have to sell on nights that are historically fully occupied? Do the math!

3. **Engage Front Desk and Reservations.** Know the reservations window for the summer and the walk in potential. Let them in on the trends mentioned at the beginning of this article. Set up a system with them to monitor rate resistance. Give them an incentive to book reservations and walk-ins at your best rate of the day—make sure when you enter the hotel and before you leave, that they know what that rate is for same day reservations and walk-ins!

4. **Stay on Top of the Internet Channels.** If you have a merchant agreement, and it is strongly recommend for independent hotels, use the extranet to cut off allocations when you reach a certain occupancy percentage, no more than 80% is recommended, for all dates going forward through the end of the summer. Also, ensure that your page placement is on the first page for the dates you have available. An associate at one of the channels indicated that it doesn't matter much as long as you are in the top 15. Check your position and allocations against forecast every day.

5. **Check the Offers and Reservation Functionality of the Web Site.** The web site is the most cost effective reservation channel—make sure it is fully functioning every day! Studies indicate that there is a huge percentage of travelers that go to the Internet distribution channels but do not buy there. They check out what hotels are at that destination at what rates and then go to the hotel's web site. Make it easy for them to buy on your site—how many clicks does it take for a guest to make a reservation? If the reservation function on the site does not interface with the PMS in real time, how long does it take them to receive confirmation?

While there are many other components of a good revenue management and distribution strategy for independent hotels, these are five daily disciplines that can be implemented immediately to maximize the revenue opportunities from the demand in your market.

The advantage of the independent hotel is the flexibility to adjust pricing strategies and control rates and inventory faster than their franchise counterparts—be one of the fast that eat the slow!

The Jigsaw Puzzle—The Fit of The Revenue Management and the Group Sales Piece

April 2, 2007—A recent study by HSMAI and PhocusWright suggests that the meetings market will be very strong in 2007. However, they also indicate that "Groups and meeting inventory and rates must be centralized and well integrated into other core systems, including hotel property management, revenue (yield) management, central reservations, customer relationship management, e-commerce and dynamic packaging."

The study goes on to say that meeting planners are using more internet platforms to locate the venues and pricing. In another study by the same company, it was indicated, "… this year for the first time online transactions will account for over half of all U.S. travel bookings."

Typically, the management of online distribution sites was the territory of the Revenue Manager and group bookings was the domain of the sales department. It would appear that the two have converged—it is even more important than ever for the two pieces of the puzzle to have a seamless interface.

The sales department has typically focused their efforts with clients and potential clients on personal relationship building. This is the first time that there is statistical documentation of customer behavior to indicate the relationship with the hotel is likely to begin without any contact from the sales department.

Group rates were a negotiated piece between the sales manager and the planner—not necessarily kept secret but hardly transparent either. The new study would seem to suggest that group rates would have to become more transparent to the consumer if they are to be loaded into e-commerce platforms, central reservations and Internet meeting sites.

This requires the seamless integration of sales and revenue management strategies and tactics. That sounds good but how do you actually execute this at the property level?

- **Identifying the E-commerce Group Sites.** The first step in the group sales e-commerce strategy is to get over the shock of not having to take every prospect to lunch. Imagine how much expense money you will save! The second is to locate group e-commerce sites and evaluate the logistics of becoming a presence on them.
- **Group E-commerce Sites by Market Segment.** Not all of them may fit the revenue management strategy in terms of the demographics of the customers and price sensitivity. The landmark e-commerce sites like Expedia and Travelocity's Groople may be a good beginning for certain kinds of groups such as social. RFP sites such as StarCite are used by a different demographic of meeting planner.
- **Integrating Internet Group Channels into the RM Strategy.** The potential revenue contribution of each group distribution channel must be evaluated. This is difficult when some of the group channels are relatively new and new to the property's group sales effort. The rate and offerings by revenue period will need to be monitored closely—by sales or the Revenue Manager. This process will probably be more art than science initially!
- **Weekly Sales and RM Meetings.** A key agenda item of the weekly Revenue Management meeting is to evaluate the contribution from all channels. As groups that use the internet distribution sites are booking into the future, it is critical to build a feature into the channel reports that allows the Revenue Management committee to see and evaluate the channel from which the group booking originated when it is consumed. This is necessary to evaluate the positioning on various channels and how to tweak it to reflect the revenue management strategy for that period of time.

The implication of this potential paradigm shift for both the sales and revenue management departments is huge! It changes how we market to groups from a strictly personal contact model to creating a group sales identity online that is compelling. It involves revenue management more intimately with the group sales function. Did anyone feel the earth move yet!?

Feeding the Revenue Elephant—Hotel Revenue Management Summer 2006

Hotel Revenues this summer are anticipated to be gargantuan—high demand and high rates. What more could an hotelier ask?

A lot! Hoteliers who blindly accept the demand that comes their way at the rate they ask will never know how good it could have been had they fed the elephant of hotel revenue with guests that were not measure solely by rate but by value.

Amitava Chatterhjee in the upcoming edition of Hospitality Upgrade has an excellent article that states, "… a 2% increase in customer retention is equivalent to a 10% reduction in costs." He goes on to say that "… hospitality enterprises (should) start measuring and tracking a guests profitability ".

How much money are you leaving on the table? How many of the customers that you get this summer at the rate you are asking will never return? How many of them are not the demographic that will feed the revenue elephant in the future? How much does it cost you when you squeeze out the high value customer for the 'one night stand' at a higher rate? What is the cost of constantly appealing to those customers without the potential to return?

So what does this have to do with Revenue Management—everything! Most revenue management proponents, (including me—see past articles on this subject) advocate measuring the value of a guest not just in terms of room rate or REVPAR but also in terms of potential for other profit centers such as F&B, the spa, other attractions within the hotel or facility.

This is a revenue management function. The more sophisticated revenue management systems can drill this down relatively easily. For those of you who are doing it the 'old fashioned way' it isn't impossible—just a bit more work.

- **Capturing the Information**. This is a training issue with the front desk/reservations. Many GMs say 'I tell them to do that'—there is a huge difference between 'telling' and 'training'. Email addresses offer a fast, cheap and easy way to cement guest relationships. There are several points at which you can capture this information—ask at check in or check out or on a 'permission' box on your web site.
- **Email Guest Comment Surveys**. This is a rationale for asking the guests for their email addresses upon check in or departure. If you are not using this medium now, it is readily available through companies that perform this function or easily accomplished by someone who is relatively familiar with technology. The studies indicate that guests are more likely to respond to email surveys than to a survey mailed to them (let's see—fill it out, put in an envelope and mail—who knows where the mailboxes are anyway—and for what benefit to the guest?) The survey also contains a section where permission is given to receive occasional promotions from the hotel.
- **Capturing the Identity of Guests Booked by the Distribution Systems**. Who are these people? (This could get me in serious trouble with my friends at some of the larger portals—you know who they are.) The guest that arrives and departs that has booked through a travel portal is invisible to the hotel in terms of market segment or demographics unless we capture the information at check in or check out. If we can get them into our system, we can develop relationships with them.
- **The Functionality of the PMS System**. Most PMS systems are capturing guest information that can then be sliced by demographics such as when they stayed, for how many nights, total bill at checkout, etc. The problem is that many hotel GMs and DOSs aren't aware of this or how to access it. This info can be use to target certain guest demographics at times of the year when they are most likely to be making reservations. It can be used for all market segments and the promotions can be used for email postcards and flyers or mailings in the absence of email addresses.

Many of you are now thinking that this involves CRM, Customer Relationship Management. This is a term that either provokes the 'glazed over eyes' or total 'brain lock' for many hoteliers. When I mention determining the 'value of a guest', many find it difficult to get their minds around it. Most of you are now thinking, "It's summer, I'm too busy to worry about this stuff". Capturing the information now will enable you to use it later

Most franchises focus their efforts on their frequent guests for whom they are able to collect this information relatively easily. However, there is a segment of guest, such as leisure, that may not be a member of the frequent guest program but whose business is valuable and can be targeted from the property level. If you are waiting for the franchise to do all this work for you, you are missing the boat.

This is especially critical for independent hotels. I work with many independents. The CRM process is not difficult but needs to be thought out and become a part of the overall marketing and revenue management strategy.

It is the most 'valuable' guests that feed the Revenue Management elephant most profitably. The cost of CRM in feeding the elephant is far lower than the cost associated with most of the other reservation channels.

Revenue Management 2006—The Risks and the Rewards!

I know that you are out there—the ones who will address that nagging worry in the back of their mind after the holiday hoopla is over—can we really achieve that budget in 2006?

The answer is yes and no—there is no reward without risk. If ever there ever was a year with a little wiggle room for taking risks in your revenue management strategy, this is it. Your staff will be looking at you for your risk tolerance and they will follow your lead—what will it be?

I know a GM who took a big risk with a citywide convention and refused to accede to their demand for a huge rate reduction accompanied by assorted comps and, oh yes, then there were those sponsorships they were requesting. All of the other major players in his market had knuckled under and taken large blocks at greatly reduced rates. He chose not to.

His rationale was that he could maximize his rate and occupancy in displaced business by not acceding to demands that would have compromised his budget for that month. A month prior to the citywide group's arrival, he didn't have a lot of reservations, two weeks out he was still dead in the water. Panic began to set in but he knew his transient reservation window was very short lead.

Reservations began trickling in and then came the deluge after the displaced reservations realized that his hotel was about the only option during that time period. At the end of the day, he filled his hotel for that period at a rate $12 higher than the comp set—need we tell you what it did for his REVPAR. His boss called him to congratulate him for making such a good call—but it could have gone the other way!

There is a saying in the theatre if you want to be noticed move when everyone else is standing still, stand still if everyone else is moving. Being a contrarian is risky but has its rewards. Try the following with your staff—

- **Stop Filing Your Revenue Glass From the Bottom Up!** Quote your higher rates first—you can always come down. There is a sentiment, outdated but still there, that we should reward our early reservations with a low rate—why? How many discounted reservations do you take well in advance of the arrival date that would have been willing to pay a higher rate? Take the risk—let your revenue manager know that it is all right to take a risk and adjust if demand patterns warrant it.
- **Quote Higher Group Rates.** Let your salespeople know that it is all right to hold the line in rate when negotiating. Teach them to sell the value and monitor their competition. If they lose one along the way don't yell at them. Train them how to fill their sales funnel with higher revenue prospects so that they aren't so dependent on that one piece of business. Let them know that some of those lower rated 'old stand bys' may need to go 'bye bye'.
- **Give the Front Desk Clear Directives.** Let the front desk know that they can hold the ground on rate and admit to you that a few people walked. Even if they go down with a few unoccupied rooms the first time or two, they will learn that it is okay to take calculated risks and they won't get their wrists slapped over it. Both you and they will get better at building value and closing walk-ins at the right rate the more you practice.
- **Encourage Your Staff in Creative Risk Taking!** In all areas of the operation, encourage your staff in all departments to be creative in finding solutions. Some will work, others may not— but we learn more from our mistakes many times than from our successes! Taking a risk and succeeding is an incredible rush!

The real risk in '06 is not to take the risk—to be conservative and do business the way you always have. Demand, rate tolerance and relative lack of new supply is providing the 'perfect storm' for creative revenue management solutions. We may not have this opportunity in 2007 as more supply comes into the market.

Go ahead—Go for it! Happy 2006!

Revenue Management and Group Sales—The Partnership not the Disconnect!

Groups and conventions are booming—a significant increase over previous years. Competition is stiff and the window to submit proposals is shortening. Evaluating the quality of a group booking for all profit centers is critical.

For those of you with sophisticated revenue management systems this process is not as difficult as for some hotels that are doing revenue management the 'old fashioned' way and there are more of those than you might think—even among large group houses and companies!

However, even some sophisticated revenue management systems struggle with the integration and analysis of the value of catering revenue and it's impact on the overall revenue management strategy. I often hear that catering revenue has a high cost associated with it and is therefore not as important as rooms with a lower cost. Until someone develops a formula for evaluating the cost of room sales from all channels as a factor in revenue management decisions, catering revenue must be considered.

Sales managers now not only have to sell the client or meeting planner but also sell the revenue manager on the 'worthiness' of a piece of business. This has always been the case to some extent but it is more critical than ever that sales understand the revenue management strategy and process.

We have discussed in prior articles the tension and sometimes (sometimes?) disconnect between the two departments. That is not the issue here—it is the partnership of the two functions that will produce the greatest maximization of revenue for the property. It is imperative that we get beyond REVPAR and evaluate the revenue potential for all profit centers, not just rooms.

Below are a few considerations for sales managers to evaluate a group if you don't have a sophisticated revenue management system to work with. In making a case for a specific group whose rate may fall at or below the RM parameters but has a significant impact on the other profit centers requires research and diplomacy. It is also a valuable process when you want to make a case for an 'exception' for a group.

- **Evaluate Past Revenue History of the Property.** Pull the revenue history for all profit centers, rooms, catering, F&B outlets, spa, etc., for the past two years. Were there groups in house that influenced this revenue and, if so, what was the revenue profile of the past group in terms of room rate, etc.? How does the current group's revenue contribution compare to previous groups? You will also need to source the rest of the sales department in relation to group bids others may be working on for the same dates and which may have better overall revenue potential for the hotel.
- **Understand the Revenue Goals of Each Profit Center.** Here is where diplomacy plays a major role. Each profit center may become an ally if you know how this group is going to make a significant contribution to their revenue goals for the period. Helping other departments get what they want is a great way to get what you want.
- **Obtain the Group's Past History.** Most companies and organizations know exactly what they spent on this meeting or similar ones in the past in terms of rooms, F&B, catering, etc. If the history varies significantly from what they have told you they anticipate, it should set off a 'red flag'—ask them why they believe this group or meeting will be different from past ones.
- **Qualify for Future Potential.** This requires that you completely qualify the account for future business prior to booking this group. Be careful—it's like the contractor who went to purchase 5 refrigerators for a development he was building but told the salesman he needed five hundred. The salesman put together his best deal. The contractor took only the five and never went back for the other 495. We've all been on the short end of this tactic at one time or the other. If they are asking for concessions on this group, tie it to a contract on a future group—have them sign both contracts.

- **Be Prepared to Walk Away.** This is a tough one. Good salespeople love to book business and then there is the question of the quota and/or bonus for the period. The faster you walk away from a piece of business that is not aligned with the hotel's revenue management strategy the faster you can move on to other prospects. In addition, if the bonus or incentive system is not aligned with the revenue management strategy, and many are not, it is a huge source of contention and the source of the 'disconnect' between sales and revenue management, therefore making the sales person even more reluctant to walk away.

The incentive system should reward revenue (notice I said revenue and not rooms) booked during opportunity periods at a higher value than business booked in peak season. It doesn't take a great deal of talent to sell business in periods of high demand and, if the bonus is based on rooms not revenue, that business may be sold at a lower than optimal rate and still be rewarded. Total disconnect with the revenue management strategy!

Disconnect—Aligning the Revenue Management and Sales Strategies

It became apparent at a recent Revenue Management conference that not only is there a "disconnect" between the sales department and revenue management but at times, it manifests in outright frustration.

I was the "token" sales person at the conference. Following my presentation on Sales and the Revenue Management Strategy, it became apparent that I had touched a nerve—that not all was well in the relationship between Revenue Management and Sales. However, the Revenue Managers in attendance expressed a sincere desire to bridge this disconnect.

The Revenue Managers' frustration stemmed from a perception that sales only wants to sell "discounted" rates at inappropriate times, doesn't understand and/or support the revenue management strategy and is primarily concerned with their "bonus" or incentives versus the revenue of the entire hotel. YIKES!

While I believe that this is not a universal sentiment—it was sufficiently pervasive to prompt this article. The role of revenue management and the sales function should be complimentary—the two strategies interlocking like pieces of a jigsaw puzzle. I was surprised that in so many cases this is not happening.

There are several areas of "dis-connectivity" that can be identified:

Inappropriate Discounting. It is easy to forget that until the last perhaps twelve months, the industry was pulling out of a deep recession characterized by decreased demand and heavy discounting by hotels in an effort to stimulate demand that wasn't there. This is a mind-set that is difficult to change when it has been SOP (standard operating procedure) since 9/11, almost four years ago. Couple this with meeting and travel planners who were dealing with drastically reduced travel budgets and hammering salespeople to give them their best rate. As ADRs increase, those same planners are again "hammering" sales for the best deal they can cut. Discounting the rate is an easy sale to make—building value into a rate and presenting it as a "good deal" takes a skill set where many salespeople haven't been trained.

Bonuses and Incentives. It is easy to make a bonus when demand is high by discounting groups. It is much more difficult during periods of low demand when even discounting probably won't stimulate additional bookings. The issue however, isn't totally the sales department's fault—it is a question of how management has structured the incentives and bonus plan. A bonus and/or incentive plan that is weighted in favor of rewarding bookings in periods of low demand and less lucrative during high demand periods can offset this issue.

Driving Revenue Across Multiple Profit Centers. This is a specialty that sales brings to the revenue management strategy. Hypothetically, midweek is the high demand period for higher rated corporate transient business but is slow for social and other catering functions and may be the slowest time for the spa. By discounting the room rate a few dollars, a group may bring high catering and food and beverage revenue as well as utilization of the spa during slow periods.

Interface of Sales and Catering Bookings and Revenue Management Strategy. Most sales and catering programs now have the revenue management metrics built into their sales and catering contact management programs. However, the potential always exists to "override" the system. It helps if the sales and catering system interfaces with the

PMS system and the RM system as the evaluation can be made in "real time" rather than when the metrics were entered, perhaps months before.

Building and Maintaining Relationships. As most of us know, every relationship is built upon the ability to give and take—even when it is not always convenient! This is no less true in relationships with clients than it is in personal relationships. Sales brings the strength of profitable client relationships to revenue management strategy. However, there are times when valued clients ask for special favors that may not always be in sync with the revenue management strategy. This can be a test of the relationship between revenue management and sales—sometimes each department needs to trust that what the other department is doing is in the best interest of the hotel.

There is much more that can be said about this issue and much dialogue that should take place between departments and management. These conflicts are resolvable with training, imagination and bonus structures so that each department is rewarded in the same way—based upon the total revenue of the hotel.

Revenue Management—The Challenge for Hotel Sales

Robust Revenue Management systems have been the drivers behind the industry's ability to drive ADR and REVPAR in 2004 and will continue to be the drivers for the foreseeable future. Consider the following forecast from PKF.

Demand is expected to increase by 2.8%. Supply is anticipated to increase by only 1.6% but ADR is forecasted to increase by a whopping 4.7% resulting in an average REVPAR increase of between 7.7 and 8.4% in 2005. "In 2005, ADR will be the main driver of REVPAR improvements," says (R. Mark) Woodworth. (Mr. Woodworth is the Executive Managing Director of the Hospitality Research Group of PKF Consulting, author of Perspectives on the Road to Recovery, US Lodging Industry 2005, HRG/PKF, HotelOnline, November 2004.)

In a typical urban/suburban mid level corporate transient property, the mid-week peaks are dominated by business travelers whose rate sensitivity is less as they, individually, are not paying the bill. While corporate travel departments are continuing to try and manage the cost of travel, the reality is that in prime locations, room rates are increasing and they find themselves negotiating higher rates in their RFPs than in previous years.

Another factor to consider is that bookings from all electronic sources have increased another 30-40% from 2003. This includes all channels from the GDS systems, e-commerce channels and the franchise web site. These bookings are also driven by an increase in leisure travel that has been induced by the lowest airfares in a decade. While airfares remain low, this segment demonstrated in the summer of 2004 that they were willing to pay higher hotel rates than in past years.

The dilemma for hotel sales departments is to locate and manage group business to fill in the blanks mid-week and weekends, often from market segments and demand generators that press for lower rates.

They also are dealing with third party meeting planners attempting to negotiate the best (read lowest) rates for their clients.

The Revenue Manager is pressing for a higher rate, group booking contacts are pressing for lower rates and the sales person is under pressure to meet their booking goals—it is a stressful situation for the sales department!

The solutions are varied but hinge upon the ability of the sales person and department to understand and be able to measure the impact of potential bookings and rates upon the hotel's revenue management strategy. Once they understand those parameters, they can then align their new business development activities in relation to the client profiles that fit the revenue management model.

It is both the lack of understanding and/or the inability to measure their potential contracts prior to negotiating and booking that provokes the criticism that "sales only wants to book the lowest rates." My firm belief is that they will stand their ground if given the tools in order to, first of all, develop new business in line with the revenue management strategy and secondly, measure the value of a group to the hotel's top line. In other words, understand the difference between good business and bad. The following are a few suggestions:

The Revenue Management Strategy. Those who are involved in developing the strategy have "buy in" to its successful execution. A hotel company that I work with has taken the position that they want to reduce the number of locally negotiated rate contracts and increase the rate on the remaining ones in order to drive a higher ADR in the mid-week period which is the period of the greatest ADR potential. Sales is fine with the understanding that their ADRs for groups during the weekends will remain the same as the past year and maybe even be a bit reduced in order to attract SMERFE business. It is a deal that is cut so that everyone knows what the expectations are. The Revenue Manager is part of the sales team rather than a direct report to the Rooms Division.

Develop Client Profiles for Each Rate Period. In order to be more effective in locating prospects that will fit into the management, it is imperative to know what you are looking for. In other words, which types of groups in market segments and sub segments will fit within the rate and catering parameters that will align with the revenue management strategy. Attempting to meet these goals through only responding to telephone inquiries and working the trace files is insufficient to attain the goals. First of all, there is no control over the kind of prospects calling and the pressure builds to respond to their requests if this is your only means of prospecting. Secondly, the accounts in the trace files may or may not be in alignment with the new revenue goals in terms of rates and meeting configurations. A client profile should be driven by market segment, where the bookings are likely to originate, their rate sensitivity or history and their meeting configurations. For example, in the SMERFE market, a group of wine enthusiasts may be less rate sensitive and more inclined to spend money on F&B than a group of students. A group originating in a city with a higher ADR may be less rate sensitive than those that originate locally.

Develop a New Business Development Strategy. Once the client profiles are developed, it becomes a matter of developing a strategy to locate and qualify these prospects. Strategies might include using the Internet to locate certain organizations within a market segment from a specific geographic location or getting on an email distribution list or mailing list for organizations that have the potential to produce groups for the hotel is another one. There are web sites that specialize in producing leads for groups for hotels in various market segments. These can be sorted by geographic location and often give the rates, meeting specs and history of where the group last met. www.grouperleads.com is an example of one of these. No strategy is complete without an action plan for implementation.

Provide a Group Revenue Management Tool. A revenue management tool can be as simple as a spreadsheet of the group rooms budget by month into which the parameters of the group can be entered so that the sales person can see how the number of rooms at the proposed rate effects the room revenue of the entire hotel for the period. It can be as sophisticated as a computer program that measures the revenue of a group on all profit centers. These take various forms and often are included with the sales contact management system such as the ones offered by Delphi. Some of these products interface with the property's PMS and Revenue management systems.

The future of the hotel sales is in being able to first of all locate groups that fit the revenue management strategy and secondly, measure the viability of a group in the date ranges and rate requested in relation to the hotel's revenue management strategy.

Engineering the Revenue Management Strategy

Why would the development of a revenue management strategy be important prior to the marketing plan development—and why is a revenue management strategy different from the budget?

A revenue management strategy that incorporates all of the revenue drivers such as GDS, the web site and the electronic distribution channels is key. However, it requires the involvement of the sales department and all other profit centers of the hotel. This is unlike a budget in that a revenue strategy is renewable and adjustable where a budget is usually written in stone.

A sound revenue management strategy includes the optimum revenue mix and the tactics to achieve it—this is where the marketing plan comes in! "Managing" revenue is just that—it assumes an element of control in the revenue that you accept from various sources based upon cost of reservation, commissions, etc.

A revenue management strategy establishes "target" numbers to be achieved through a variety of ways; sales, manipulating the GDS, controlling the allocation and rate in the electronic distribution channels, etc. In other words, it is a pro-active rather than reactive function that simply turns the faucets on and off.

The sales strategies in the marketing plan flow from the revenue management strategy although sales is critical in developing it. The sales department is critical in that they have their fingers on the pulse of the market. They are responsible for assembling the economic information on market conditions and analyzing the potential threats to the market as well as identifying the opportunities. The sales department knows the potential of each market segment and the rate that each one will bear.

The development of the revenue management strategy allows sales to gauge how many rooms in a given period they can book by market segment and at what rate. It also insures that existing and future group blocks won't be sabotaged by lower rates on the web site or distribution channels.

How exactly should this process work?

Gathering the info: Each member of the team, but especially sales, should have been keeping information in regard to the market such as trends indicated by the STR reports and other industry sources. Sales should take the temperature of top accounts to see what their forecasts for travel next year look like. The group logs pace reports for this year and next year should also be put into the file. Sales should also have the situation analysis completed as well as identified challenges and opportunities for the upcoming year.

Analyzing the Revenue Data: The revenue reports should be analyzed to indicate the percentages currently generated by all revenue drivers. This, of course assumes that the data is accurate. If anyone has any doubts about the importance of proper market segment coding by reservations and the front desk they should end here. It is "GIGO" (garbage in—garbage out)! If there aren't accurate numbers, you will be playing a SWAG game (I am not going to explain that one).

The Facilitation: This is the meeting of the minds, GM, sales, reservations and any other interested party such as the owner. They take a look at the budget, market conditions, all sources of revenue, etc. and begin projecting the revenue strategy by segment. This can be a contentious process as the sales department fights for accounts and room allocations by rate. However, as an associate once said, harmony is vastly overrated. This process can take several days as all of the evidence is presented and numbers are plugged into the model and adjusted—yada, yada. It never hurts to have an outside consultant facilitate this process to provide objective third party input.

The Final Product: The spreadsheet, created from compromise that fulfills the requirement of the budget, becomes the basis of the revenue strategy. Every revenue driver is identified and the ideal mix of revenue and rate is there to yield the targeted REVPAR. Every revenue driver in the revenue strategy should have its own strategy and tactics section in the marketing plan—including the web site, the GDS strategy and the electronic distribution channels (don't make the mistake of leaving it up to the franchise).

The Review Process: The same fractious group that designed the strategy should meet periodically, it could be monthly or quarterly, to make adjustments based upon reality. In the initial development, "triggers" should have been identified that would automatically call for adjustments. Those triggers include unanticipated market changes, good or bad, changes in the economy and any national security breaches (God forbid!).

It's a "messy" process, but a necessary one for the marketing plan to be developed. It then becomes the road map for the coming year. The marketing plan is not just about sales but the revenue management strategy for the entire hotel.

"A dynamic marketing plan must include the strategies and actions for generating and managing revenue across all the revenue channels—sales, electronic distribution channels, the web site and include the revenue management and CRM strategy as well. Learn how a marketing plan can maximize all of the opportunities that present themselves in a recovering economy." Carol Verret

Hotel Revenue Management this Summer

—a Game of Skill, Art and Most of All Nerves

Recent studies by several respected research firms indicate both good news and reasons to be cautious about the 2004 summer travel season. Both the TIA and Yesawich, Pepperdine, Brown forecast an increase in leisure travel for 2004. TIA forecasts an increase of 3.2% over 2003, which is an improvement although certainly not stunning given last year's lackluster performance.

Yesawhich and partners indicate that 33% of leisure travelers anticipate more trips this year compared to last year while 38% intend to take about the same. Twenty-nine percent expect to take fewer trips. Both of these surveys are good news for hoteliers.

Two other surveys, while not conflicting with the above, offer a few cautionary tales for hoteliers. The Myvesta Summer Vacation survey of 1000 adult Americans conducted May 14-16 indicates that the average American is planning to spend 5.3% less this year than last year on summer vacations. With the rising cost of gasoline, guess where they will attempt to trim their spending.

In addition, Yeaswhich and partners research on the use of the Internet in travel planning by leisure travelers indicates that 63% use the internet to plan travel and 45%, up from 32% in 2002, will book travel services online. This indicates that the leisure traveler will compare price and product to make their decisions.

Many hoteliers, flushed by this surge of good news and an opportunity to recoup some of their profitability from a lackluster 2003, are rushing to push rates. There is an inherent danger of pushing rates too far and too fast, especially on the part of those hoteliers whose market share penetration is languishing at or below 100%.

It is imperative to remember that REVPAR is a combination of both occupancy and rate. An ADR index often rises in inverse relation to market share penetration when rate is driven too radically thus leaving the REVPAR needle unmoved. In addition, it is important to retain positioning in the market, especially as it is presented on the electronic distribution channels.

If memory serves, we were seeing some of the same trends in the forecasts for 2003—more leisure travel and more price sensitivity. The trend was derailed by the war in Iraq and a stagnant economy. While the economy is showing bright spots, the stock market is waffling, the war continues and the price of gas is escalating.

It is at this juncture that revenue management becomes a game of skill, art and most of all nerves. It is a high stakes game. There are several variables to consider in playing this game:

- **Market Share Penetration and ADR Index.** Ideally, the market share index and ADR index should be tight. That is, the percentages should be within a few percentage points of each other. If market share is well over 100% (110% or more) the hotel should be pushing rate but be prepared to lose to a certain number of market share penetration points. Decide in advance how many percentage points you are prepared to decline in market share. When you reach that hurdle, leave the rate level. If you are below that market share threshold, drive rate very conservatively and be prepared to back off when you get rate resistance and denials.

- **Position on the Electronic Distribution Channels.** If you are well positioned on the EDCs in terms of rate and product don't be lulled into a false sense of security. The positioning needs to be checked and evaluated with more frequency given the short lead times we are now experiencing. This is the only way to maximize the seasonal opportunity. In periods of high demand, adjust rate and inventory allocation on a daily basis if necessary. This also applies to the franchise web site. Check your positioning in relation to the other franchise products in your market—the select serve hotels are well positioned to take market share from full serves in a price sensitive climate.

- **Check the Pulse of the Market Daily.** If you have access to Day STR reports, use them and analyze them every day. Have the night audit drive to work fifteen minutes earlier and count cars in the competitors lots as well as note any tour buses or other marked vehicles. By keeping your finger on the pulse of the market every day, you can adjust course and remain nimble in the reservation system, EDCs and rates quoted across the desk for walk-ins. Blind shop the competitors every day for their walk-in rates.

- **Gamble Based on Calculated Risk.** Don't be too cautious—overbook on high demand nights but do so based on facts. What is the average no-show factor for that night of the week under similar conditions; look at last years demand patterns. Those who don't examine and learn the lessons of their past history are doomed to repeat it!

- **Listen to your Revenue Manager.** If you are fortunate enough to have a revenue manager who attends to all of the above, analyzes the numbers and makes recommendations—listen to what is said. It is tempting to put someone in an advisory position who tells you only what you want to hear. It is equally tempting to have someone who will tell you what they think and then disregard it when you don't agree. Ask for the facts and figures but don't filter out the ones that point in the opposite direction of what you want to believe.

It is not my objective to throw cold water on positive exuberance, but there are some warning signs in the positive trends. Disregard them at your peril. Make money but don't jeopardize your long-term revenue potential for the sake of the summer season.

The Memorial Day Weekend will give us an indication of what lies in store for the rest of summer season. Enjoy it and may it be the beginning of a positive trend!

Revenue Management: The Integration of Revenue Drivers

As peak season nears for many hotels, revenue management is the key to a successful summer season. Leisure remains strong even as business travel continues to disappoint and it is imperative that in March the pieces are in place to maximize revenue.

Potential customers are much smarter than they used to be about locating, qualifying and making their hotel choice. In many cases, this process is completed without ever contacting the hotel.

The term revenue management means many things to different people—whatever the definition, the intended end result of the process is increased REVPAR for the organization. It is increasingly clear from feedback that I receive at seminars and from my consulting clients that there is often a lack of co-ordination and/or consultation on the rate and offering through all of the revenue drivers.

Revenue drivers are defined as all areas of revenue generation within the organization. This includes central reservations, property-level reservations, the sales department, the electronic distribution channels and the web site. While franchised properties have a higher level of consistency through the GDS, it still requires monitoring and management at the company or property levels.

At a recent sales seminar, participants expressed frustration that they are largely unaware of, nor are they consulted about the rates that are posted on the electronic distribution channels. One result is a very high attrition rate in meetings and conventions as attendees book their hotel at these lower rates and "fall" off the group block. Another consequence is when the rate posted is lower than what has been negotiated with third-party suppliers such as wholesalers.

A coaching client of mine expressed frustration over his lack of consultation in the development of the new property web site and the rates that are being quoted through the site. First of all, the content was skewed to a specific market segment that was not representative of the core business segment and secondly, the copy changes disrupted the optimization strategy.

Thirdly, the rates that were quoted were not at all aligned with the rates being quoted at the property level or through the central reservations agent and many room descriptions were inaccurate. The end result was that not only was this hotel nowhere to be found on the key word searches in the major search engines—a potential disaster for this independent property, but fewer reservations were being made through the site.

Collaboration across all departments that generate revenue is the only way to ensure continuity. This need not be a tedious process of endless meetings. A few things put into place and adjusted periodically, based on market conditions and forecasts, are sufficient:

- **Product/Rate Positioning**: A plan for product/rate positioning is ideally developed as part of the Business/Marketing plan process and includes consideration of the product/rate positioning of the competitive set, group bookings, rate resistance input from reservations and past history. Once the strategy is developed, it then only needs to be adjusted periodically. Don't forget to monitor the franchise yield management system in light of groups or events in previous years that may not be a factor in the present year.

- **Existing and Anticipated Contracts**: These include group contracts, volume contracts with LNRs, wholesalers and any other rate commitments. Just as the sales department makes decisions based on the rate structure, so should consideration be given to any agreements made thorough sales. It is one thing to adjust rates on the web site or distribution channels to drive volume at a slow time but if it undermines the agreements above, it is counter productive.

- **Web Site Presence and Reservations**: Many leisure customers locate the hotel through key word searches on the search engines. Others locate the hotel on the electronic distribution channels then access the hotel's proprietary web site. Still others will pick up the phone after visiting both and call reservations to see if they can cut a better deal. It is essential that the "message" of rate and offering be relatively consistent across all channels to be effective. The rates on the web site need to be adjusted in tandem with the electronic distribution channels and reservations needs to be aware of what's appearing on both.

Another consideration in web site development is the increased use of the site as a sales tool. It becomes the electronic brochure. The sales department's inclusion in its development is essential to the site's secondary role as the electronic brochure. Salespeople should be accessing the site with their clients to moderate the virtual tour. If there is a special rate posted that is inconsistent with the rates sales are quoting, it blows them out of the water and appears to the client that the hotel doesn't know what it is doing.

The process of collecting the information is about communication and collaboration and can be accomplished through periodic updates from the revenue drivers to the revenue management team. This swings both ways as revenue management needs to keep the revenue drivers informed of their proposed tactics in order to solicit input and buy in.

The consequence of not doing this is to present an inconsistent message to the public who is in the position of making selections without any direct contact with the property thus depriving the hotel of any opportunity to make adjustments or explain the disconnect. In the consumer's mind, a hotel that can't get its act together to project consistent rates may have the same problem when it comes to servicing them as guests.

The issue is more than rate parity, it is aligning the rate structures between all revenue generating departments so that each is maximizing their contribution to revenue.

Triple Witching Hour—The Marketing Plan, Revenue Management Strategy and RFPs for '06

It's triple witching hour in the hospitality industry! Let me explain—it is the time when the marketing plan, RFP bidding and establishing the revenue management strategy all combine into a confluence of factors that will influence success in 2006.

The term is adapted from the stock market and is defined as follows:

"An event that occurs when the contracts for stock index futures, stock index options, and stock options all expire on the same day. Triple Witching Days happen four times a year: the third Friday of March, June, September, and December. This phenomenon is sometimes referred to as "Freaky Friday." The final trading hour for that Friday is the hour known as triple witching hour."

Fortunately, our triple witching day or hour happens only once a year if we have addressed and aligned our strategies in these three areas. But this is critically important to fiscal 2006.

At times, these three strategies are developed in a vacuum—uncoordinated and when this occurs one of these departments, revenue mangement or sales, is compelled to 'knuckle under' to the other. This is easily addressed if the sales and revenue mangement strategies are developed in concurrence and harmony (yes, I said harmony!)

I have addressed the issue of the 'disconnect' between sales and revenue management previously. It does not need to be this way and I will outline how we can avoid this conflict and move the property forward to where it needs to be to take advantage of the tremendous opportunity that this recovery in our industry is experiencing.

1. RFPs. Sales often fills out the RFP forms without checking and comparing actual rate and productivity in relation to arrival/departure patterns, displacement of higher rated business and seasonality. We are so often eager to capture the business—any business—that we fail to remember who signs our paycheck. If the RFP business pattern is not aligned with the revenue management strategy, we sabotage the RM strategy by blindly accepting the terms and conditions of the consortia and other RFP requests.

What we fail to remember is that these contractors are in the business of pushing for the best deal they can get and most of them have admitted that this year that they know it is a 'sellers market'. Our job in sales is to know the parameters of the RM strategy so we can push back and negotiate the best deal for the hotel. Remember, these contractors would like to have but do not need to have 'last room availability'. A 'win-win' is optimal but not necessary.

2. The Marketing Plan and Sacred Cows. I am a sales person by training and nature so I know where you all are coming from in this regard. We all have 'sacred cows', those accounts that have been with us forever and to whom we are loyal, whether it is because they are nice people to deal with, give us free passes to an event, you name it! However, from time to time and this is one of those times, we need to re-evaluate with an unemotional eye the business and rate that these accounts are seeking in relation to the revenue management strategy.

It is often helpful to bring them into our strategy and allow them to tell us theirs so that we can decide if we can forge a deal that works for both the hotel and the account. If not, we have to understand that it isn't going to work for the hotel and look for new business that will. It is way too comfortable to remain with the old standbys so we don't have to engage in that messy business of prospecting for new accounts.

The marketing plan initiatives should support the revenue management strategy. For example, if a discount promotion is planned has it been conceived in conjunction with the revenue manager and does the expiration date coincide with the revenue management strategy?

In terms of sales strategies, does every sales person understand the rate parameters for quoting groups for days and periods of time in '06, '07 and forward? Is the new business development strategy aligned to focus on prospecting for business in each market segment that will interface and compliment the revenue management strategy? In each market segment, there is business that is more value driven and less rate sensitive than other business—yes, even in the SMERFE segment (another article, another time.)

3. Developing the Revenue Management Strategy. In developing the revenue management strategy, the Revenue Manager looks at a number of historical variables in order to anticipate demand. The goal is to provide the right product to the right customer at the right price at the right time. Isn't this also the goal of sales and marketing?

The revenue management strategy should be developed in tandem with the sales and Marketing Plan for the revenue stream to move forward most profitably. Both departments should be rewarded accordingly.

A great deal of the tension between the two departments will disappear if the sales incentive structure is changed to reward the sales department for revenue during 'opportunity' or off peak periods. It doesn't take a great deal of talent to sell discounted business during high season.

When all of these processes are aligned triple witching hour becomes the time when revenue is optimized for the hotel. It is truly a wonderful thing when a 'plan' comes together!

Revenue Management Systems—Considerations for Evaluation

A recent Cornell University Study found "hotels that price above their local competitors to be the most aggressive revenue managers. (This study)—also suggests that those hotels which are best able to extract high REVPARs are most likely to engage in revenue management practices." (Cathy Enz, PHD, Linda Canina, PHD, The Center for Hospitality Research, Cornell University, Analysis of Revenue Management, Vol 5, No 6, April 2005.)

Most (not all) hotels want to be able to sell rooms at higher rates resulting in increased REVPAR. If aggressive revenue management is the key, as the article suggests, many will be looking to institute or upgrade their revenue management systems.

As many of you will go to HITEC and look at the latest in revenue management systems, it is good to stop and pause prior to being seduced by the most sophisticated technology. It is prudent to establish exactly what the requirements of the hotel are in terms of functionality and how an RMS system can make the process more effective resulting in increased revenue.

The needs of a 100-room boutique hotel are quite different from those of a 900-room hotel with multiple revenue sources such as F&B outlets, catering revenue, spa, etc, and a large group component. A hotel company with several hotels within a geographic area has different requirements than a national company with hotels spread across the country and no two of them in a close proximity.

In anticipation of implementing a new system or upgrading an existing one, some criteria should be established in order to evaluate the potential ROI of individual Revenue Management Systems and their suitability for the objectives of one hotel or a hotel company.

One company that I know of is doing this by assembling a team of key staff members from the corporate office and managers of different departments from selected properties. Their mission is to develop a framework for identifying the key functionalities expected from a Revenue Management System and a blueprint for implementing it. This gives each property and department a role in defining the objectives and expectations of the system and so should encourage buy-in from all of those that the system will impact.

Some of those evaluation criteria are:

Who needs to know what and why? In other words, what does each department want to see in terms of reports and other pertinent data in order to make decisions? What is the minimum required by each department and what is the optimal requirement?

The Current Revenue Management System. If you currently have a revenue management system, why are you considering replacing it? Is it all of the system that you want replaced or are there certain functionalities that you would like to "add" to it? Is it more cost effective to start from "ground zero" or to purchase "add ons?"

Channel Management. Most systems do this adequately. How sophisticated a system you require is dependent upon the complexity of your business mix. Will the system allow you to evaluate different channels revenue streams or are all of them dropped into the same basket?

Managing Multiple Revenue Sources. How well does the system manage and evaluate revenue from unique revenue sources? For example, a property with a water park in addition to the usual hotel revenue sources needs to be able to manage the park's revenues effectively and evaluate business that maximizes revenue to all departments. A property with a popular spa needs to evaluate how the revenues of both are interrelated and manage both the inventory of rooms and spa services.

Analyzing and Predicting Customer Behavior. How will the system incorporate customer behavior into its forecasts? Can it provide reports of customers' decision making timelines by market segment so that Marketing can use it to target campaigns? Will the data enable Customer

Relationship Management to catch the repeat guest at the right time with the right offer at the right price?

What are the Benefits for Smaller Properties? Is the system under consideration "scalable"—can some parts of the system be implemented without purchasing more functionality than necessary? Will the benefits deliver an appropriate ROI on the investment? Will the modules of a new system interface with those of the system already in place?

Will the Corporate Office Have Access to the Individual Hotels' Systems? In many companies, the situation exists where the skill sets of the property Revenue Managers vary from hotel to hotel. Will a system "level the playing field" allowing the corporate revenue manager to support those properties whose managers are less proficient?

How Will the System Evaluate Group Business? Many salespeople complain that they have been relegated to booking groups only on the weekends and the revenue managers conversely complain that sales only wants to sell "cheap" rooms. How will the system enable the sales department to make good group bookings that satisfy the requirements of the hotel's revenue management strategy and the sales persons' desire to meet their goals? How finely can the system "drill down" the data to enable the decision making process in RFPs and contracts?

Can the System Manage Demand within a Geographic "Cluster?" Some hotel companies have multiple properties within close geographic proximity to each other. Can a revenue management system assist in the redistribution of demand so that all of them can maximize their revenue based on geographic demand?

You will notice that the above section has more questions than answers. That is due to the fact that the answers are up to the buyers and those answers will make the difference in purchasing the right system at the right price or being dazzled by technology that may be more than the hotel requires and therefore, provide disappointing results. The process of arriving at the answers is almost as important as the answers themselves given that it is the process that will determine if the new system receives "buy in" from all of the departments that "need to know."

General Managers Managing the Sales and Revenue Management Process and User Generated Content

General Managers have their hands full with the operation and now they are expected to understand all of the recent developments in sales and revenue management as well as understand UGC (user generated content). They have to deal with becoming a 'green' hotel and managing three generations in the workplace—Baby Boomers, Gen Xers and Millenials.

When I was VP Marketing for Sunstone Hotels, I never quite understood why my DOSs wanted to become GMs. GMs are responsible not only for top line revenue but bringing it to the bottom line, managing the managers and interfacing with irate guests.

For this they get to be on call 24/7, keep the peace among warring managers and report to both the management company and the owners. GMs need to know a little bit about everything.

The articles that follow hopefully help give the GMs a little bit about the new processes of sales, developments in revenue management and how to use online reviews to motivate their line staff!

GMs—How User Generated Review Sites Can Make you a Better Manager!

User generated review sites are the ultimate mystery shopping experience—only they are free! This is the guest speaking directly to you and the staff—this is better than a comment card. It is easy to be critical of the review sites just as the industry has had a love/hate relationship with the online travel agencies.

It all began with Trip Advisor that engendered the same reaction from many hoteliers as the online travel agencies did when they first arrived—platforms that many loved to hate. Neither Trip Advisor, the online travel agencies or Web 2.0 are going away—they will only become more dominant in how our customers find us, research us and ultimately select their travel and hotel arrangements.

If one has followed the studies primarily at the beginning of the year, they confirm this trend. In a recent survey, Yahoo Travel found that 61 percent of people now go online for vacation recommendations. In addition, the study suggested that a property's reviews replaced price as the deciding factor in hotel selection. Travelers are no longer just searching for a hotel based on price; they are now making decisions based on user reviews, user ratings and photos.

The line between review sites and Online Travel Agencies is now totally blurred—review sites are becoming OTAs and the OTAs are (and have been for a while) user generated review sites! The industry just didn't pay a lot of attention to the reviews on Travelocity, et al, until Trip Advisor came to the conclusion that since people were selecting hotels based on the reviews, it may as well let them book hotels while they were there.

How can user generated reviews make you a better GM?

- **Guest Service.** Print and discuss all service related issues at staff meetings. Use the reviews to coach and mentor department heads and employees. Use positive reviews as a recommendation to potential associates that you are interviewing for employment—everyone wants to work for a winner! When you post responses to a review, print those out to indicate that you are responsive to what guests are saying about your hotel and that you take guest comments seriously.

- **Monitor Operational Deficiencies.** If an issue is recurring in several reviews across several sites, that constitutes a trend—take action! Rooms that are perceived as less than clean, persistent maintenance issues, front desk processes—engage the staff in brainstorming solutions. If a video is posted of an area with a deficiency, show it at staff meeting. This way it isn't personal coming from you—it is coming straight from the guest who recorded it. Set an incentive for reviews that are good and fail to mention previous operational issues.

- **Revenue Management.** Don't just monitor your reviews, have your Revenue Manager monitor the reviews of your competition! This is a window as to how your competitors are perceived by their and potentially your customers. If your reviews are consistently better than those of your competitors, is it an opportunity to enhance your standing in the competitive set and even increase your rates? When you are positioning your hotel in the competitive set, don't forget to include the reviews of each of them in your positioning exercise. TravelClick has a new tool called SearchView debuting in October that allows you to see not only your reviews but ranking with your competitors and it sorts the types of reviews by operational areas.

- **Sales and Marketing.** The GM is still the CMO—Chief Marketing Officer of the hotel. Use the status of good reviews on Trip Advisor et al, in promotional emails to your customers. Incorporate your standing on the review sites as a third party recommendation to close the business. This can be your trump card to beat out the competition when rate and offering are similar to a competitor whose reviews are not as good as yours. Get up to speed on how your hotel is positioned on the small group booking sites as well as the meeting planner sites.

- **Recommendations to Owners.** If a capital expense issue is consistently mentioned in reviews and illustrated by photos and videos posted about your property, you have a good third party reference as to why you need to make physical changes. Justify your Capital Expenditure request with the videos and photos. Quote and/or show them the studies of the influence of these sites and estimate how much revenue this issue is costing them.

Don't fear the influence of these sites—make these sites a management tool to assist you in making your operation better—and the best news is they're FREE!

Revenue Management for Hotel GMs: What You Don't Know Can Jump Up and Bite You!

General Managers have vastly different levels of understanding the revenue management process. In this year of opportunity, what a general manager doesn't know and understand can jump up and bite him or her you know where. The levels of understanding tends to range from "I don't really know what the Revenue Manager does all day" to those GMs whose background was revenue management.

If you as a GM fall into the first category or anywhere close (and you know who you are), a speedy ramp up on revenue management is critical to your property maximizing the revenue that ultimately becomes the basis for your bonus or incentive. The gaps in your RM skill set can jump up and bite you in the wallet—how's that for a WIIFM* factor!

There is a feeling on the part of many GMs that Revenue Management is simply the old yield management concept repackaged. Yield management is part of it but it is far more complex than that and advances in the discipline are morphing at light speed.

Revenue Management is more complex than ever and changes in the discipline are morphing at light speed. RM not only manages demand during peak periods but also has a huge impact on stimulating demand in shoulder seasons. RM no longer only applies to room revenue but to managing the potential revenue for all profit centers. It enables a smart Customer Relationship Management strategy that has the potential to stimulate demand from the most valuable guests.

The position of the General Manager is one of juggling competing priorities, keeping the department heads from seriously hurting each other and at the same time trying to produce an exceptional guest experience. What's a GM to do to ramp up the Revenue Management IQ? Below are a few areas to test your RM IQ.

- **Understand the Reports.** Your Revenue Manager probably produces a plethora of reports and proudly gives them to you during the Revenue Management meeting. (You do have a weekly Revenue Management Committee meeting, don't you?) The reports come from various sources including the PMS, the GDS, the various channels and franchise reports. The Revenue Manager has probably designed a few of their own. Stare at them until they begin to make sense, ask for explanations and don't pretend that you understand them when you don't.

- **Daily, Weekly and Monthly Disciplines.** This is key to understanding what your Revenue Manager does all day. There is a set of activities that need to be performed at these intervals. Know what they are—how else can you measure how well the Revenue Manager is executing the RM strategy.

- **Channel Management.** We now refer to channels as all sources of reservations. If you still think this refers only to the Internet travel sites, you need to ramp up. Managing these channels is more than just turning the inventory and rate faucet on and off, it also includes merchant agreements, internet specials, GDS marketing etc, to stimulate demand. This is a critical area for your Revenue Manager.

- **Web Site.** Especially if you are managing an independent hotel or resort, you as a GM need to understand site design, optimization and Internet marketing. This is critical to the success of any independent. Your Revenue Manager should be intimately involved with the design and functionality of the reservation engine on your site.

- **Rate Strategy versus Pricing Strategy.** The rate strategy is where you position your rate structure for the year or fiscal period. The pricing strategy includes closing discounts, rates for 'hot dates' etc., in the short term or within the period covered by the rate strategy.

- **Revenue Management and Customer Relationship Management.** This tends to produce the glazed over 'deer in the headlights' look. The simple explanation is that CRM is about identifying the value of customers, individually or by market segment and then developing relationships with them in order to secure their loyalty or, put simply, repeat business. It can be this simple or much more complex but GMs need to understand what this means and the implications for the future.

The above is a short list of some of the basics that all GMs need to have a grasp of even if their Revenue Manager is supported by a Corporate Revenue Manager—remember it is your hotel's revenue for which you are ultimately responsible and compensated for. For those of you who don't know what the WIIFM factor is it is the acronym for What's In It For Me—I hope we made that case!

The GM'S Role in Revenue Management

At a recent regional General Manager's meeting, I was invited to facilitate a discussion on the revenue management process and the GM's role. There were seven General Managers in the room and we had about as many opinions on the subject.

The opening comments ranged from not quite knowing what the Revenue Manager actually did all day to viewing the Revenue Manager as setting policy on the rates to be quoted by everyone in a position to do so—with a lot of comments in between. Some viewed the Revenue Manager as a gatherer of data only and the position as being essentially a part-time function while others viewed the Revenue Manager as critical to the overall revenue strategy of the hotel.

I would hazard a guess that the answer is variable, depending upon the company and the hotel policy. What was evident in this discussion was that some GMs had a higher comfort level with the Revenue Management process than others.

The relationship between the sales department of the hotel and the Revenue Manager is another potential area of confusion. In some situations, Directors of Sales have indicated to me that there was little communication between the two departments. Many times group blocks were sabotaged by a lower rate that the Revenue Manager had offered to the Electronic Distribution Channels, incurring a high attrition rate for groups whose attendees had located that lower rate for the hotel on the Internet and booked out of the block.

One DOS indicated that her staff had to get approval from the Revenue Manager prior to quoting rates for groups. It was often difficult for the sales person to explain a lower rate quote for a certain period of time justified by the organization's potential to book more business in an opportunity period, the need for rate consistency within a market segment, or a long standing relationship that the organization had with the hotel.

How does a GM lead the Revenue Management process to ensure that both the needs of the client and the hotel's revenue objectives are met, not to mention ensure the cohesiveness of the team?

Understand the Revenue Management Process. Many General Managers are uncomfortable with the process because they simply do not fully understand it. The discipline of revenue management has morphed over time with many new systems and programs available. Take a course on up to date revenue management. There are many offered on the Internet that are both time and cost effective. You cannot manage the process unless you fully understand it.

Develop an open attitude about the Electronic Distribution Channels. Back off, take a deep breath and consider the following: 1. These are reservations that your front desk or reservations staff does not have to process, 2. You have been paying a commission to Travel Agents since the beginning of time anyway and 3. You don't have to offer them a dirt bag rate! While recently assisting a client in the development of the hotel's revenue management strategy, it became evident that the ADR for these channels in one high occupancy period exceeded the hotel's ADR by $5 (after commission). Why? Because the hotel had let them pull the rate from the GDS during a period when all low rates were closed. By understanding this, you can make these electronic channels a valuable part of your revenue management strategy.

Establish a Revenue Management Strategy. Simply put, this means establishing room and rate allocations by market segment and opportunity dates and seasonality for the year, to be reviewed quarterly. This should be an essential part of the marketing plan developed in collaboration with the Revenue Manager, the sales department, front office and reservation managers and anyone else whose department is affected. Be prepared for heated discussions as everyone makes their case for their "pet" market segments. Make it clear that if sales or anyone else wants to give a lower rate to a group or segment in a given time period, the revenue must be made up in other segments.

Conflict Management. Expect conflict. As a wise person once said to me "Harmony is vastly overrated." While I am not suggesting that you tolerate a prolonged battle zone within the hotel, the dynamic that arises when people have conflicting but justifiable views benefits the process. Create a framework for managing revenue management conflicts when they arise and establish a decision making process—even if that means that you cast the deciding vote. Leadership is not a popularity contest!

Be prepared to take risks. Revenue Management is not an exact science. Be prepared to take risks yourself and encourage the "risk takers" on your staff, provided that they can provide valid reasons to take them. You will win sometimes and sometimes you will lose. Example in point: A General Manager I know decided to vote against becoming a host hotel for a certain group and not to offer the preferred rate with the comp rooms that the group was asking for. His was the only hotel in the market not to do so. The "last to fill at the highest rate" strategy is always a risky one. A week prior to the group's arrival, they were sitting pretty much dead empty, the anticipated demand no where in sight and the GM was sweating bullets. At the end of the day, or night in this case, the hotel filled at a rate $25 higher than the rest of the market but it could have gone either way.

Leading the revenue management process is critical to the success of the hotel. It is not about analyzing the data within the spreadsheet but is ultimately about creating value for guests in every market segment without jeopardizing the hotel's revenue goals—it is that guest value quotient that we often lose site of in the process!

Leadership—General Managers Managing the Sales Process

General Managers are being asked more and more often to assume responsibility for management of the sales staff. It is a job for which they have received little training and for which they have a number of challenges.

Five years ago, when demand was high and the sales function was relegated to answering the phone and taking the order, it was relatively easy for General Managers to keep an eye on things in the sales department. Unemployment was at historic lows and in order to keep positions filled, we were reluctant to expect too much or discipline an under-performing employee. There was a tendency to keep the chair warm rather than let a position go unfilled.

Times have changed both on terms of demand and the employment pool but often the attitudes of management have not. Salespeople represent a distinct management challenge. The good ones are bright, aggressive, able to sell their managers as well as their clients but they are also very human.

They like most other employees will take the path of least resistance, need to have expectations made clear and have objective standards of performance by which they are evaluated. The fact of the matter is that no one does what no one checks!

Salespeople (like everyone else) do not perceive the importance of job duties that are not monitored by their supervisors. In addition, there has to be the WIIFM factor, 'what's in it for me'. If an employee, sales or not, is going to take home the same paycheck whether or not they achieve their goals, why would they do more that the minimum requirements?

GMs have a particular challenge in that they work long hours and very closely with their sales staffs, especially the DOS. It is difficult to maintain an objective and professional distance that allows for the kind of management that gets results. We all have a human need to be liked—leadership is about respect.

There are a few simple steps you can take to make your monitoring of the sales effort more effective. They may also make the sales effort more effective.

Refrain from Cronyism—Simply put, this means do not get too close to your DOS or any member of the sales department. (You wouldn't compromise your ability to lead the other department heads by too much socializing—or would you?) It is difficult with a DOS who has worked for you for a long time. It is also difficult with the long hours required working in close quarters in this industry. There has to be a line of familiarity that you don't cross. It negates your ability to lead and manage effectively. You know when you have crossed the line. Weekly golf games are probably too much as is frequent social sharing of coffee or drinks. I know a GM whose VP of Sales, the VP of Ops and TWO consultants indicated that the problem with the turnover and lack of effectiveness of the sales department was the DOS. He still didn't listen. When this particular DOS took another DOS position with another hotel within the company, he lasted less than two months. The GM had worked with this DOS for several years, they played golf once a week and he frequently had the DOS and spouse for dinner at his house. It totally blinded him to the persons deficiencies in job performance and the DOS took complete advantage of the situation.

Have regular sales meetings with a fixed agenda. It should occur at least once a month, preferably once a week at a time when it does not interfere with Prime Selling Hours. (You do know what those are, don't you?) This provides a structured environment in which you can ask the 'tough' questions without sounding picky and irrational. I have had GMs say to me "but we talk to each other several times a day—I know what's going on." To a sales person, if you just casually ask a question about an account or ask for numbers, they are likely to feel that you are just in a bad mood and it will pass. In a more structured environment, you can ask specific questions about accounts mentioned on reports, question the content of numbers on the PACE report, etc. There is an old story, perhaps apocryphal, that Kurt Carlson, the founder of Carlson Companies, used to ask his Division Heads to bring their financials on overheads. He would project pages on a screen and point to one specific number line item on the page. He would then ask what was in this cumulative number. He figured if a Division Head could specifically outline what this represented, they knew and could do the same on any line item in the reports.

Take a course in sales. If you come from another discipline in the industry, learn about basic sales. Read a book, take a course—take a course in sales not related to the industry. Many of the best hotel salespeople I know come from outside the industry where they were on a commission basis at one time or another. Remember when I said if a sales person (or any other member of the staff for that matter) draws the same paycheck whether or not achieve call and or revenue goals—why would they do ore than necessary to achieve their goals. (A great argument for incentives for all departments but that is another newsletter.) There are many fine resources for hotel sales available especially now when that function has become so challenging. We hope this newsletter is one of those. Salespeople who have worked on commission 'get it'.

Set realistic goals and involve them in the process. Goal setting should be an objective process. When you let them know what they need to produce and why, then involve them in figuring out how they are going to get there, they understand and ideally buy into the plan. If they don't buy in they will begin to float their resume. I have had salespeople whine to me about unrealistic goals. I have been in that position myself. We all have choices—if they feel it is unattainable, they can exercise their choice to walk. If they are really good salespeople who feel that unrealistic goals have been foisted upon them, they will do exactly that. You need to let them know that if you feel the goals set by the corporate office are unattainable, you will go to bat for realistic goals given the market circumstance. You have been around the block enough times to know the difference between a challenge and the unattainable.

Be supportive but expect results! Your head is on the line here too!. If your sales staff is making a ton of calls but producing few results, it could be a skills problem. Offer them some training. When a reasonable amount of time and training effort has passed, don't be afraid to make the tough decision. The fact of the matter is they are uncomfortable at their non-performance and may be happier and more satisfied in another position. As a relatively new DOS, I had a GM whom I admired and respected indicate to me that I had to deal with a non-performing sales manager. I argued, I whined until he said, "Carol, one of you is going—it's your choice." Message received.

I could continue but that is a whole seminar. The message is don't expect to be loved by every member of your staff every day—settle for respect on good days!

Independent Hotels and Resorts

Web 2.0 and its impact on hotel sales and revenue management have gone a long way to level the playing field for independent hotels and resorts. The internet is the great democratizer and the positive comments on the review sites can't be bought.

In the area of search, franchises and independents can enable SEO strategies and Pay Per Click campaigns so that when a potential guest searches for a property in a specific market, both have an equal shot at coming up on the first page. In the Web 2.0 world of user generated reviews, many independents are becoming higher placed than their franchised sisters due to their uniqueness.

Independents may not have the resources available to them that their franchise counterparts have and have to source them on the open market and pay for expertise. However, in exchange for this they don't have the fees and restrictions that franchise organizations impose on their franchisees.

Over the past few years, many hotel guests have come to appreciate the uniqueness of independent hotels and resorts as well as boutique hotels. There is a small rebellion against the 'cookie cutter' boxes where everything is pretty much the same, especially in the leisure travel market.

While franchises have been quick to develop new brands that attempt to replicate the hip boutique experience within the franchise environment, many of these new brands simply become tomorrow's boxes where everything is pretty much the same although certainly 'hip'.

In the world of online RFPS, independent hotels have an equal shot and often are preferred by meeting planners for their uniqueness.

Independents need a healthier marketing budget to craft their online presence. However, when a market turns down or an initiative doesn't work, the independent hotel and resort can make a fast turn and either pursue a different direction or make adjustments to the strategy. The ability to do a complete 180 degree course adjustment in the sales or revenue management strategy gives them an agility that their franchise counterparts envy.

Here is to that spirit of independence!

Five Revenue Management Tactics for Independent Hotels

"It's not the big that eat the small, it's the
fast that eat the slow"
(Jennings & Houghton, 2005).

For independent hotels that's good news. Independent hotels and resorts may not have all of the resources available to them that their franchised counterparts do but they have the advantage of greater flexibility—independents can gear up or down in a flash!

There are some challenges ahead this summer that need to be monitored for their impact in specific markets. PriceWaterhouseCoopers has predicted that 2007 summer will be a record year for the number of occupied hotel rooms; however, "… The summer occupancy in 2007 is forecast to be slightly lower than 2006, 69.6 percent, … and approximately a percentage point below the 70.2 percent occupancy in 2006."

In addition the study goes on to say that the price of gasoline is finally taking a toll American's travel habits. "… The price of gasoline will result in approximately 8,000 fewer occupied rooms per night, or 0.2 occupancy points." An 8,000-room decline spread nationwide does not appear to be a lot but for hotels that operate in markets that are seeing significant new supply, the impact on the market will be more profound.

As the demand number becomes more delicate, it was inevitable that "there is also emerging price resistance following hotel average daily rate increases of 5.5 percent and 7.1 percent in 2005 and 2006."

There are five basic revenue management tactics that independents can implement to be nimble and responsive in the face of changing demand and rate patterns:

1. **Check Pricing Strategy Against Last Year's History.** How many fill nights on what days of the week in the month

did you have last year? Are rates adjusted accordingly based on those demand patterns as well as this year's groups, special events, etc? Do you have the nerve to be the last to fill at the highest rate?

2. **Close Discounts.** This may be a no-brainer for some but many hotels leave their 10% discounts open such as AARP and AAA. The rationale is that it is only 10%—how much is 10% on a rate of $100 times the number of rooms you have to sell on nights that are historically fully occupied? Do the math!

3. **Engage Front Desk and Reservations.** Know the reservations window for the summer and the walk in potential. Let them in on the trends mentioned at the beginning of this article. Set up a system with them to monitor rate resistance. Give them an incentive to book reservations and walk-ins at your best rate of the day—make sure when you enter the hotel and before you leave, that they know what that rate is for same day reservations and walk-ins!

4. **Stay on Top of the Internet Channels.** If you have a merchant agreement, and it is strongly recommend for independent hotels, use the extranet to cut off allocations when you reach a certain occupancy percentage, no more than 80% is recommended, for all dates going forward through the end of the summer. Also, ensure that your page placement is on the first page for the dates you have available. An associate at one of the channels indicated that it doesn't matter much as long as you are in the top 15. Check your position and allocations against forecast every day.

5. **Check the Offers and Reservation Functionality of the Web Site.** The web site is the most cost effective reservation channel—make sure it is fully functioning every day! Studies indicate that there is a huge percentage of travelers that go to the Internet distribution channels but do not buy there. They check out what hotels are at that destination at what rates and then go to the hotel's web site. Make it easy for them to buy on your site—how many clicks does it take for a guest to make a reservation? If the reservation function on the site does not

interface with the PMS in real time, how long does it take them to receive confirmation?

While there are many other components of a good revenue management and distribution strategy for independent hotels, these are five daily disciplines that can be implemented immediately to maximize the revenue opportunities from the demand in your market.

The advantage of the independent hotel is the flexibility to adjust pricing strategies and control rates and inventory faster than their franchise counterparts—be one of the fast that eat the slow!

Independent Hotels & Resorts: Ride the Wave or Float with the Tide?

Okay, so you independent resorts and hotels have noticed an uptick in business—BUT where are you in comparison to the market and to last year? There is an old saying, "A rising tide floats all boats."

If you are posting only a 5-7% increase in revenue over last year, then you are only tracking the industry average. Congratulations—your boat is floating.

What's wrong with that? Nothing if bobbing around in the water is all that the owner expects. But let's think about this. A "floating boat" has no forward momentum and the level of the tides that ebb and glow dictates its "level."

So do you want to float or do you want to have the ability to "steer" this boat regardless of the tide—ride the highest wave? Do you want forward momentum that puts you in control of the property's revenue and destiny?

There are cost-effective ways of positioning your independent hotel and resort but they must be co-coordinated. The following is the bare bones of a targeted plan:

Rate and Offering Positioning: First of all you must decide on a rate structure in relation to your position in the market with your competitive set. Who is your competitive set? That will vary depending on the type of facility, location and season. For example, I had a client, a resort whose competitive set was other lodging facilities in the area for meetings in the off-season, but whose comp set was regional and national for leisure travel in the busy season. The same client however, believed her rooms were worth the same rate every day of the week, every month of the year. Your room is only worth what your target guest is willing to pay—and that may be a lot less in January in the northern part of the US versus what they are willing to pay in July.

Revenue Management Strategy: What will your revenue management strategy be? Revenue management for a small property may be as simple as a spreadsheet with formulas so that you can manage the inventory in a Best Available Rate block allocation. If you are a mid- to large sized property, invest in the best revenue management system you can afford. You will see a healthy ROI if you put an internal system into place. You will also want to determine who will manage the yield on a daily, weekly, monthly basis? Which leads to the next section.

Property Management System: The investment in a good PMS system is worth every penny. However, most property management systems can produce the reports and the data you need to manage the property. The issue is how well does the current staff know the system. Often a system was installed and training was given on the basics and finer points of the system but only the basics have been passed on and no one is left who remembers where to locate the denials/regrets reports, how to harvest mailing labels or email addresses for Customer Relationship Management, etc. Call the provider and ask if there are updates for the system that you can purchase and upgrade to the best functionality you can afford.

Web Site and Search Engine Optimization: Just because your nephew, friend or friend of a friend (fill in the blanks) creates web sites, resist the urge to call them! One hotel I know followed this strategy and eight months later was waiting for corrections to be made because the web site developer had to get a day job! An entire book could be written about this subject but in brief—find someone who specializes in the hospitality industry— there are many good ones. First and foremost, it is about functionality not art. The ability for a potential guest to check availability and make reservations in "real time" is revenue waiting to flow into your hotel. Make it easy for people to give you money! Key words and links should be decided upon before the copy is written and need I mention accurate web traffic reports?

GDS Presence and Reservations Capability. One of the wisest investments you can make is to hire a company to provide 800 number reservation services and GDS placement that will be picked up by the E-commerce channels. First of all, you probably are expecting the front desk staff to service the guest and sell reservations at the same time. Bad idea! Many of your desk staff may be hired because your local labor pool is limited and they could smile and fog a mirror not because they are good at sales. Even if they were, you would have to spend more time and money training them to do that on a continuing basis to compensate for turnover. Additionally, when the phones are the busiest for peak season reservations so is the hotel.

Group Sales: A well planned group sales effort can support your property in the off-season and maximize revenue in peak season. A thorough examination of revenue drivers with one client led us to promote weddings in the peak season on weekends as the rooms were guaranteed at a high rate AND the average per person banquet price was $86 per head, not including alcohol, which flowed freely at this destination resort as no one drove home. Could we have gotten a higher room rate—yes, slightly, but could we have replaced $10,000 to $15,000 of banquet revenue per weekend? Not likely.

The above is only the tip of the iceberg. I have one client of an independent whose case study I would have liked to include but I couldn't reach him to ask his permission—he is too busy handling 92% occupancy, up from less than 40% last year. He is riding the wave—not floating on the tide. Enough said!

The Challenge of Marketing Independent Boutique Hotels

We all have wonderful memories of a charming hotel in which we stayed that was free of the cookie-cutter image, had an intimacy that made us feel special and nooks and crannies that invited us to linger and relax. Hoteliers often harbor a retirement fantasy that when the mainstream career comes to a close, they will walk into the sunset and operate an inn or a bed and breakfast and will have gone to hotel heaven. Well, let me tell you that hotel heaven can turn into hell very quickly.

Because of their size, small boutique properties often do not have the clout in the market to recruit and retain good line employees. Seasonality can have the happy retired hotelier making beds, doing laundry and unstopping toilets in the off-season when he/she has had to lay off the seasonal staff. Any furloughs due to seasonality pretty well guarantee that the quality labor in the market will go to a property with the mass to offer them year round employment.

Budgeting and forecasting can be a nightmare if accurate records of the previous years are not kept. Benchmarking performance in the market is difficult due to lack of access and the expense of Smith Travel Research reports. Overhead and expenses can run high when the market dictates rate ceilings. The PMS systems available to independent hotels often lack the sophistication of those available to franchise properties. Inventory management is critical to maximize revenues in smaller properties and the available tools often reside in the manager's brain.

If this scares you off then you should doing something else. The rewards are the opportunity to create a guest experience based upon hospitality rather than efficiency, to implement customer service that makes memories rather than horror stories, to truly be in touch with guests rather than seeking to avoid them because a guest contact usually indicates a problem.

Marketing an independent boutique hotel requires a certain finesse and accountability due to the restrictions of size and budgets. As there is no franchise driven marketing program and its accompanying contribution to occupancy by virtue of a GDS system and 800 numbers, nor is there a frequent guest program, the marketing plan has to be developed and executed with precision accuracy to reach the potential guest with a true appreciation of a boutique hotel and the ability to pay the price for this level of service and intimacy.

There are several key factors to develop a lean and targeted marketing plan for boutique hotels:

Begin by developing a client profile for each market segment by season. This should also include the F&B outlets. The profile should be developed demographically, geographically and fiscally. Only when you have a clear picture of your guest can you target both sales and marketing efforts and media placement. Sign up for the reservation and marketing systems available to independent hotels that best reach your client profiles. Track their production so you can review performance and make adjustments in your selection if necessary.

Use electronic distribution channels and manage the heck out them. Have a dynamite but easy to navigate web site that is capable of accepting reservations online. Ensure that your web master has you entered in the search engines by key words that appeal to your guest profile and pay for them to regularly refresh your web site positioning with the search engines. Use email to advantage when your site includes an email response capability.

Develop a Public Relations Plan within your marketing plan. The GM should be the point person for this so the sales person(s) can be dedicated to selling. The GM should be heavily community involved and serve on key committees where the visibility is highest for the target guest and/or can have access to and participate in the formulation of civic and tourism policies that benefit the hotel. Become a patron of a key charity that has a high profile with your potential guests.

Develop your own Customer Relationship Management program. Collect as much information about your guest as possible. Not just the name and address but the kind of wine they had with dinner, events or attractions that they booked through the hotel or the hotel's concierge such as theatre tickets, special events or festivals and last but not least, whether they liked feather or foam pillows. Many years ago I was a Sales Manager with The Four Seasons Hotel in Montreal when the company was still small enough that Isadore Sharp would come and sit in your office and ask how things were going. The reservations department staff took all reservations by hand but we had a computer with a customer relationship management program (although we didn't know to call it that) that was state of the art. We knew the answer to the pillow question and if the guest preferred Evian or Perrier. These things were done prior to the guest checking in.

Develop cost effective mailing pieces targeted to past guests and potential guests that your profile for the period of time or promotion that you have developed. Back to the bottle of wine in your CRM system! If your or F&B outlet or an organization in your community is sponsoring a wine festival, search the CRM for the information and mail your promotional piece to them.

This may sound trite but MAKE SALES CALLS BASED ON YOUR TARGET CUSTOMER PROFILES. For example, what segment of travel within a company appreciates and has the travel budget to utilize your facility. Who are they and how can you gain exposure to them. Which types of associations match your client profile in terms of demographics, geographic and the fiscal resources of their members?

There is so much I could say and do! It is fun marketing these independent boutique hotels because it does require a certain creativity and finesse to reach those target markets within budget. The rewards are in knowing that when the hotel is successful it was a team effort not reliant on the power of a franchise.

The next six to nine months could be difficult for independent boutique hotels. As many of them do not have access to deep pockets, let us all sincerely hope that we don't lose too many to closure or franchising. It is these unique qualities and the experiences that they enhance (as well as the retirement fantasies) that make the contribution of boutique hotels to the industry so valuable.

A Shot of Customer Service

The hotel industry essentially gave up trying to produce a consistently great guest experience at check in and check out. That is why many hotels are using kiosks. They justify it by saying that the guests requested it. The guests requested it because we couldn't get it right!

The fact of the matter is that we don't treat the people that provide the guest experience with enough respect to pay them a living wage and offer career paths. If we are lucky, we hire enough people with the right 'attitude' that can be trained. Those people stay for maybe a year if we are lucky. Then the process starts over again.

Hoping that we get 'lucky' is not a good strategy! The training for the front desk is heavy on technical knowledge of the PMS system, the steps of check in and check out and light on guest service skill sets. We evaluate their training based on the technical skill sets acquired but are hard pressed to measure their guest service skills.

Observable behaviors that constitute a good guest transaction are measurable. For example, the concept of 'acknowledging the guest' can be broken down into 'make eye contact when a guest is within three feet of the desk', 'smile' (I know this should go without saying but don't count on it), ask 'how may I help you'.

Behaviors that are observed are measurable and provide the basis for mentoring and coaching. Build in the evaluation of these behaviors into performance reviews.

Our front line service associates are the hotel to the guest—investing in their training and resulting job satisfaction can yield benefits in terms of repeat guests and guest generated reviews!

The success of the hotel is literally in the hands of the least paid and, as a result, sometimes the least committed! The hospitality industry needs to invest in customer training for every employee that has the opportunity to have guest contact. Tom Peters wrote that the average time spent on training in America was 26 hours per year per employee; I would venture to say that in most hotels, we don't come close to that.

Do you think Tiger Woods would be Tiger on only 26 hours of training of year? How can we expect to build A service teams without an investment in training?

"Smile" is a Learned Behavior—Creating a Culture of Customer Service

I always enjoy John Hendrie's articles on customer service. His recent article on "Smile, It Enhances Your Face Value" is dead on. Unfortunately, it begs the question that many managers express to me "How do I get them to smile?"

In two other articles. The Case for "Smile" Training and Generation Y: Training a New Generation of Employees, I made the case for the "smile" and why it is important to transmit this to Gen Ys (and all the other ones we deal with). It amazes me that the Gen Y article of four years ago is still one of the most accessed on HotelOnline archives and it tells me that we, as an industry, have still not addressed some customer service training issues.

It is mid-summer and the industry is experiencing record REVPAR increases driven by rate rather than demand. The attempt by many hotels and hotel companies to install and implement check-in kiosks indicates that they have given up on training employees to give great customer service to travelers who, on average, are paying 9% more in rate than they were paying last year. (Priceline Survey, HotelOnline, July 13, 2005.)

What many hotel marketers and Revenue Managers miss is the value of the repeat customer who is driven by customer service as well as by price. It is a matter of "the value proposition"—reaching the right customer at the right price at the right time with the right product! Customer service is a large component of that "value proposition" that attracts the "right customer" to return to the hotel.

We would all like to think that we hire only those who have the right "attitude" but the reality is that few of us have a labor pool so deep and so wide that we can hire only those with the right "smile" attitude. For many of our potential employees, "smile" is a learned behavior. If the number of body piercings is relatively small, we can train the behaviors that will impress the guest.

"Smile" is a learned and observable (read evaluate-able) behavior. When we learn how to train employees in observable behaviors that we want to see exhibited to our guests, we can raise the bar on our customer service standards. "Telling" them isn't good enough—we need to demonstrate, model and measure the behavior that we expect.

Training managers to train their employees is the most cost-effective way of transmitting customer service training in high turnover positions. The following are some principles that we use in this program:

- **Hire for Talent/Train for Skill.** Talent is closely related to attitude. It is the ability of a potential employee to exhibit the "image" and empathy that we want them to project to our guests. If you were a guest, would you feel good about the person you are interviewing as a representation of the service that you will experience in all aspects of your stay?
- **Identify the Competencies/Skills.** What do new employees need to know and how well do they need to know it? Separate the hard skills from soft skills. Let them know the metrics you will be using for evaluation.
- **Make the Expectations Clear.** How many of you use a "skills training checklist" by timeline? In other words, in 30 days we expect the following level of competency in these skills, 60 days, 90 days, etc. It gives the employees a framework to measure their own skill acquisition. Put it in terms of observable and measurable competency.
- **Break Down Concepts into Observable Behaviors.** What exactly do you mean when you say "acknowledge the guest?" What behaviors does that concept entail? Hint—the first is "smile!" My favorite is "I want my employees to use common sense"—what the heck does that mean to an eighteen year old?

It is not difficult or complicated when you apply "common sense!" (YIKES, did I say that!?) I think you will find that common sense is a direct result of the experience that the manager has acquired—help your employees acquire that experience and you will find that they soon exhibit "common sense."

Generation Y: Motivating and Training a New Generation of Employees

Generation Y is usually described as that generation that comes after the Generation called X. The troubling thing is that after the next generation, presumably, Generation Z, do we go back to A or will we have to become more imaginative in our labeling of age groups. To define them a bit further, Generation Y is composed of 14 to 24 year olds.

As the labor pool becomes tighter, the hospitality industry is dipping deeper into this age group for line employees and lamenting the fact that turnover is high and service levels are low. We often have the specter of employees being driven to work by parents because they don't yet have a driver's license. The fact of the matter is that this age group is very different from even their predecessors, Gen X and even more removed from whatever the generation was before Gen X.

I have spoken to many hotel managers who feel resentment that these new employees are totally unresponsive to 'or else' motivational tactics and will leave them if they become disgruntled for the same money or another fifty cents an hour. Managers lament the lack of loyalty and unwillingness for go the extra mile for the 'team'. When confronted with a performance issue, the employee will sometimes just stare at the manager as though he or she is from another planet—in a way, the manager is from another planet if he or she is over thirty.

What's even more frustrating to some hotel managers is Generation Y's total disinterest in 'sucking up' and tendency to bluntly tell the manager and other employees exactly what they think of a situation. They don't even care if you fire them—although they will seldom give a manager the opportunity to terminate them, they just leave!

Generation Why

Well, get used to it and learn how to deal with them because they are the future and the manager that learns how to motivate them and train them will earn their undying loyalty. That is the message of Eric Chester, an author and speaker who coined the term Generation Why. At a recent speaking engagement at the Colorado Hotel and Lodging Association convention, he outlined the events that have influenced this group of employees and how to manage, motivate and retain them.

Eric speaks at schools and works closely with young people. He is also the author of four books targeted to teens and parents. This is a generation who watched adults get away with murder, literally, (remember the impact of the O.J. Simpson trial and the JonBenet Ramsey case) and who have noticed that hard work and character aren't the quickest routes to fame and fortune (think the lottery and Who Wants to Be a Millionaire?, not to mention Who Wants to Marry a Millionaire?).

Eric postulates that because their earliest influences have been television and Nintendo, they are "stimulus junkies", easily bored. They are skeptical with well-developed garbage detectors and desensitized, which means that respect isn't yours by virtue of your title. Eric says, "They crave the limelight, having noticed that fame comes to many for simply being in the right place at the right time and they are blunt and expressive. The good news is that all of this stimulus has made them adept at multi-tasking, fast thinking, passionately tolerant in terms of diversity and astoundingly creative."

Eric went on to outline eight strategies for managing and motivating Generation Why:

1. Let them know that what they do matters.

2. Tell them the truth—don't try to pull the wool over their eyes (to put it politely)

3. In order to get 'buy in', explain the 'why' of what you re asking them to do and tell them what's in it for them.

4. Learn their language—communicate in terms they understand.

5. Be on the lookout for "rewarding opportunities"

6. Praise them in public—make them a 'star'

7. Make the workplace fun

8. Model behavior—don't expect one thing out of them that you don't and won't deliver yourself, be the example.

Implications for the Hospitality Industry

While Generation Y may come from a different place, influenced by factors that are unique to them, managing them does not sound all that difficult. As a matter of fact, the eight strategies above are what good managers do and have always done. These strategies work equally well for every generation, in every organization at any time.

Managers who have succeeded to this point in managing by intimidation and threats won't make it with this generation. This is a generation that has never known unemployment. Work is there for them if they want it. They are in the driver's seat—they choose you. Money isn't the prime motivator—they can get that anywhere. Unlike previous generations that would grumble at being poorly treated but stay for the sake of a paycheck, these workers won't put up with it. Why should they? The onus is on us to make the workplace make sense to them, to keep it interesting and fun.

The smart companies do this. Others have been so overwhelmed by the robust economy, that they have not taken the time to pay attention to these basic principles of good management or they never knew them in first place. In the new economy where managers are struggling to maintain basic levels of customer service with fewer employees, it is difficult to gain a perspective that allows them to plan and execute good recruitment and retention policies, much less a customer service training program that gives them an edge. The consumer is unfortunately beginning to accept mediocre customer service as superior because basic levels of customer service are becoming increasingly rare.

Our employees not our customers are now forcing us to return to these basic and good management principles. Our employees are forcing us to recognize their status as our internal customers and to service them if we have any hope of motivating them to provide decent customer service to our guests.

Motivating and Training Gen Y (or Gen X or Z)

The above two concepts are inseparable, when you give someone the tools to do the job and make the expectations clear, they become more motivated. In reading and studying CRM (customer relationship management if you've been in a cave or working the front desk) notice that it is predicated upon accumulating guest history and preferences and solidifying the loyalty of that customer. This is based upon the premise that a retained customer is less expensive than obtaining a new customer.

While the above is a marketing truism, what the whole concept assumes is that we are providing the customer service to A) obtain correct information (garbage in—garbage out) and B) that the customer is experiencing a sufficient level of satisfaction to return. Both of these speak to the issue of customer service training. We assume that if we hire the right people, they will treat the guest well. The paradox of the present is that we may hire the right people but if we don't treat them well, they won't stay long enough to allow us to deliver a consistent level of customer service to the guest.

Let's re-visit Eric Chester's principles and add one more:

9. **Let them know that what they do matters.** When was the last time that you shared your guest service scores with your employees or read the good comment cards at a meeting of your employees? (When was the last time you had all-employee or departmental meetings?)

10. **Tell them the truth.** When did you last indicate exactly what was going on—as in we have half the house checking out today, it is going to be stressful but we can do it.

11. **Explain why you are asking them to do it.** When did you last explain to your employees that an athletic group might be difficult to serve but that it is a slow period and they account for revenue that helps the hotel achieve its budget?

12. **Learn their language.** When was the last time that you took the time to sit down and communicate to your employees, one on

one, about what they did on their day off—the things they like to do?

13. **Be on the look out for rewarding opportunities.** When did you last hear or see an employee providing good customer service and praise them on the spot for a situation well handled?

14. **Praise them in public.** How often do you use an employee meeting to praise a housekeeper on bringing a lost item to your attention so you could contact the guest?

15. **Make the workplace fun.** Have you ever brought bubble bottles to work and taken them to housekeeping just to be silly and play before they pick up their carts? This works with any generation in any language.

16. **Model behavior.** When did you last work the desk during a difficult check-in and show your associates the correct way to handle a difficult guest? Do you say negative things about guests within earshot of your employees?

17. **Give them the tools to do the job.** Why is it that our front desk, housekeeping and maintenance training is focused upon technical skills but includes virtually no training on the soft skills of customer service? Don't assume that they have empathy for the guest, know how to handle a difficult customer situation or understand what you expect in terms of servicing the guest if you don't communicate the expectations and give them concrete skills to turn basic customer service into good or exceptional customer service.

Understand and appreciate the challenges of Generation Y (Why) in order to recruit and retain this new wave of potential employees, but apply the principals to all of your employees. It's 'best practice' management and it works with all employees.

Why Customer Service Seminars Don't Work

In my last article, Creating a Culture of Customer Service, I explored the fact that poor and or inconsistent levels of customer service are the most pressing issues facing the hospitality industry and we are as an industry at a bit of a loss in addressing them. I suspect that these issues will become even more pressing when the summer's customer service scores from the franchises are complete. A sense of urgency will probably arise when corporate and property level managers, whose bonuses are in part based upon them, realize the extent to which their year-end compensation is affected. This is not to say that they don't already have a sincere interest in the satisfaction of their guests but the concern is certainly intensified when it hits them in their pocketbooks.

Beginning with Service America in 1990, Karl Albrecht and Ron Zemke postulated that for every customer who has an unresolved complaint or problem, 26 other people will hear about it first, second or third hand. That is unless they conduct customer service seminars as I do and talk to many people at a time, then hundreds of people will hear the story. Service America was closely followed by In Search of Excellence, Thriving on Chaos and other books on the subject by Tom Peters. Tom Peters said then and still is saying that if you are not serving the customer, you had better be serving someone who is.

The latest in customer service advice is provided by a thin book called "Fish" by Stephen Lundin. It is entertaining and refreshing and can be purchased with a video and facilitator's guide for conducting customer service seminars to reinvigorate the customer service at your organization. The package even comes with a cute stuffed fish.

In between, there have been waves of popular and entertaining books on the subject, most can be purchased with video tapes and the authors are busy giving seminars on the subject.

Why then in the last sixteen years, with so much written and so many seminars on the subject, has industry in general and the hospitality industry in particular been unable to provide a consistently high level of customer service?

We can point to the low unemployment rate and the concomitant problems of recruiting and retaining employees. We can site the increased sophistication and expectations of the travelling public. The fact of the matter is that customer service seminars alone do not work—their benefit is transient and declines rapidly over a short period of time. What then are potential solutions?

How then do we transmit lasting training and customer service values to the customer service providers, those that are on the front lines and interfacing with our guests day in and day out? In my last article, I offered recommendations that generated a great deal of interest but not much specificity. In this article I would like to get very specific about the elements of a continuous customer service training and support system.

The Customer Service Training System

The Seminar Components

1. The customer service seminar, while not sufficient alone, it is an essential element of the system to introduce the values and behaviors associated with customer service and invigorate and motivate the line employees. When I say line employees, I don't only mean the front desk and food and beverage wait staff. We underestimate the customer contact of maintenance engineers, housekeeping and the kitchen. The kitchen staff needs to understand the customer service parameters of the wait staff in order to serve them.

2. The train-the-trainer seminar for managers who hire, train and supervise the line employee is essential to define and solidify the values of the original customer service seminar and teach them how to hire and train the best customer service employees. When I receive poor customer service from a line employee, I never blame them—I blame their supervisors and managers for doing a poor job of training them and giving them the tools they need to serve the customer.

The Reinforcement Components

1. The line employees need to be reminded of the crucial concepts and techniques in the seminar, such as the steps for handling difficult customers. The inclusion of compelling posters in key employee areas helps to reinforce the initial training and assists in new employee training.

2. Managers struggle with various customer service and training issues. A monthly chat room or conference call with a customer service theme provides ongoing stimulation and the forum to which they bring their current challenges and issues as they relate customer service. This serves the purpose of reinvigorating them

and provides support in their day to day challenge of increasing guest satisfaction scores. Recruitment strategies form a part of this forum

3. FAQs—a location on the web or available as a handout provides a place where the managers responsible for supervision and support can gain additional information about handling difficult customer service issues and the implementation of strategies for customer support and recruiting.

4. A monthly newsletter provides examples of great customer service and successful strategies that the managers and employees can submit. This can be distributed electronically or through regular mail.

New Employee Orientation

This is the manager's tool to introduce the values and behaviors of the customer service system to new employees. This provides the foundation upon which the manager can build and gives the new employee the basic tools to 'hit the ground running' in servicing the guest. The workbook or web site includes an evaluation of the employees grasp of the material that can be placed in the employee file as a verification that the principles of customer service have been understood.

The line employee and train-the-trainer seminars should be repeated on an as needed basis depending on level of turnover. The effectiveness of the system can be embellished with employee incentives based on attaining levels of excellence as measured by franchise guest service scores on departmental basis and comment cards on an individual basis.

Without the comprehensive support and reinforcement system, customer service seminars don't work in the long term. The comprehensive system works in so far as there is commitment on the part of senior management to providing superior levels of customer service as the best sales tool to retain clients. Customer service seminars that stand alone are expensive in that they do not provide an investment for the long term without the above elements to perpetuate the intent.

As an industry, we provide support systems for managers, sales and front desk in the areas of revenue generation; a retained customer is a long-term revenue generator. How much are a repeat guest and the invaluable word of mouth recommendations that they provide worth?

Creating a Culture of Customer Service

Since so much has been written and discussed about customer service over the last decade, how is it that so few of us are getting good customer service? As the economy continues to boom and unemployment remains low, customer service is the challenge of the day. We are victims of our own success. One need not look much further than the United Airlines customer service disaster of this summer to see an example of that point. Granted, the airline is blaming the 'weather' and a pilot work slowdown. However, it took an outcry from the government to bring them to the point where they started to publicly apologize to their customers. It is not that difficult situations occur but how we handle them that count.

Books have been written on subject of customer service. Every one brings up their favorite stories of poor customer service and how much they paid to receive it. I could tell you my own United Airlines stories, so could thousands of us—each trying to 'one up' the other in terms of horror and inconvenience.

The airlines, however, are not alone in trying to manage increased load factors and still get the planes off the ground with fewer employees per customer. It is significant that now United's flight attendants are complaining of receiving poor 'customer service' from their employers.

The hospitality industry is also struggling with 'increased' loads from more guests and a shortage of employees, as is every other industry that has customers. The retail industry is seeing that people prefer to shop on line in many cases than go to a 'bricks and mortar' store to spend money and be served poorly. Is it any wonder that our guests now feel more confidence in making a reservation through the Internet than they do in calling central reservations or the hotel itself? In our circumstance, the guest still needs employees to check them in and service them throughout their stay. We don't have a way to clean rooms, serve food and beverage and check them in and out on the Internet.

In my last article, I alluded to the fact that we as an industry have done a relatively poor job of motivating and training the few employees that we do have. It is a 'chicken and egg' question of investing in training when records show high levels of turnover or can training make a difference in employee motivation and retention.

Generations X and Y can leave us for an extra fifty cents an hour if they are not motivated and stimulated by what they are doing. Many of them have never made a reservation, never been a guest in a hotel and their F&B experience is limited to fast food. They don't know what we expect in terms of customer service unless we not only make the expectations clear but also treat them as though they are our 'internal' customers and give them the level of service that we expect them to give.

Every organization has a 'culture' of values or 'how things are done'. This includes who gets rewarded in terms of recognition and promotions as well as how we treat each other, both vertically and laterally. Our employees are our customers and they will treat the guest as well as they perceive they are treated. They also want to do a good job. No one gets up in the morning and goes to work wanting to do their job poorly.

So we have two issues here:

Making the expectations clear
I find that demand for my customer service seminars has increased and is often prompted by a glaring guest problem that draws management's attention that maybe the expectations were not made clear. One example was the response of a night auditor to a guest complaint. (The hotel shall remain anonymous). This hotel management is one the best at creating a culture of guest service, from ownership through management ranks. One day, however, the auditor passed a card to the Director of Sales saying that this individual had had a problem with housekeeping and could she call the guest. Upon calling upon the guest, it seems that his problems went deeper and included the auditor's response to his complaints. After expressing his problems to the auditor, the auditor responded with "Better luck next time." The

disturbing thing is that the auditor honestly thought that this was an appropriate response. Do you know how your night auditor would respond in that situation?

Another situation arose when a maintenance engineer was summoned to a room at a mountain resort. The guest indicated that the room was too warm. The engineer responded that it would cool off when the sun went down. (Strike one). The guest then said that of the two air conditioning units in the suite, only one appeared to work. The engineer then responded that it was because the second unit was simply used for spare parts. (Strike two) The guest checked out. (Strike three—you're out). The point is that both were honest responses. The engineer was confused at the guest's irritation at his responses. I could go on and on.

Rather than providing our employees with the tools to respond appropriately to the guest, we wait until there is a problem then reprimand them at worst or counsel them at best, which feels like a reprimand unless you understand what was expected in the first place. In addition, failing to make these expectations clear and getting the employee's agreement that they understand them, leaves us open for potential liability if and when an employee is disciplined or terminated. This can be avoided through several means including a skills checklist, policy outline or a seminar outline that the employee signs as an indication of receipt and understanding which is then placed in the employee's file.

Creating a culture of customer service
If I am understanding the flight attendants correctly, their complaint is that they were not treated like 'customers' and given the support that they needed to service and satisfy the customer. Our employees treat our guests in the manner in which they are supported and treated. Our behavior toward them and each other models the behavior that our employees feel is acceptable.

If we expect them to treat a 'grumpy' business traveler with deference and courtesy do we afford the same treatment to them when they arrive to work 'having a bad day?'

I am reminded of the general manager who, in the course of a discussion in a seminar on handling guest complaints, asked what is a complaint worth in terms of compensating a customer? How much is a dead battery in the remote control worth in terms of making a guest feel better versus not having hot water? The value that we place on these is in direct proportion to the guest's level of irritation and circumstances. A broken remote control on Super Bowl Sunday ranks right up there with a corporate guest who can't get a hot shower before an important meeting. What is the dollar value that we place on customer service? Do guests paying a lower rate get a lower level of customer service? Have your employees heard you say of a guest "What do they expect for a group rate?"

If our employees hear their managers complaining about each other and sniping about demanding guests, what message does it send to them? How do they see you dealing with other employees and managers? How do they see you handle a guest complaint? Do we reward good service or simply admonish poor customer service?

Recommendations

If the problem is a double-edged sword then the solutions require a two pronged approach to be effective.

1. Provide your employees with basic training and systematic follow-up in terms of giving them the tools to serve the guest through seminars and consistent media enforcement. One on one training works only in so far as the trainer is consistent, has been trained in training and is exemplary. So often we assign a new employee to an old employee who simply passes on bad habits. Systematic follow-up is the repetition of the same message with new ideas for improvement either through newsletters or 'refresher' discussion groups. Again, seminars, follow-up and 'refreshers' need to be targeted and engage Gen X and Y.

2. Create a culture of customer service in your own organization. There are definite techniques to erasing the old ways of relating to fellow managers and employees and instilling a culture where everyone has both internal and external customers. This revolves around treating each other with the same amount of respect that you accord the guest and trusting each other to do the job. Did I neglect to mention not backstabbing or speaking badly of each other in front of the employees? This is also an issue of systematic training and support where each manger can bring his or her employees service problems and be 'refreshed'.

Organizational cultures exist either consciously or unconsciously, we can choose the culture that we want to work within and transmit to our employees and customers. A guest can feel a 'culture' within a hotel just as a passenger can tell if the airline is serious about customer service. Ask me how.

The only question that remains is what value do you place on your guests' experience?

Postscript

I need to stop now or this book will never be finished. As I generate at least one article a month and a number of blog posts I could go on forever! But the most important reason I need to stop is that Web 2.0, the impact of the 'long tail' as described by Chris Anderson, Editor of Wired Magazine is impacting the hotel industry at warp speed.

The developments impacting the hotel industry are rapid and exciting. I am excited about the 'green' movement in terms of making hotels less polluting and contributing to improving the environment. I am excited about the trends in boutique and independent hotels—both the hip and the historic.

I am excited about the rise in university programs to professionally train future hotel managers. The dynamic of having three generations at work in the hospitality, each with a unique sensibility, brings vitality to the industry that it hasn't enjoyed before.

I am excited about the belated recognition of the impact of the travel industry in general and the hotel industry in particular has upon the economy. Tourism and hospitality have the potential to rescue many third world countries in terms of generating jobs and tax revenues.

I am excited to be a part of this industry and grateful for all the opportunities it affords me—to travel to clients in other countries on other continents, to see every state in this country except one (I'm not telling!). I am excited to be part of the change in this industry!

Printed in the United States
133803LV00006B/228/P